Irina's
Inspirations
for Jewelry

Irina's Inspirations for Jewelry

From the exotic
to the everyday

Irina Miech

KALMBACH BOOKS

Kalmbach Books
21027 Crossroads Circle
Waukesha, Wisconsin 53186
www.Kalmbach.com/Books

Published in 2011
15 14 13 12 11   1 2 3 4 5

Manufactured in the United States of America

ISBN: 978-0-87116-402-5

Editor Mary Wohlgemuth
Art Director Lisa Bergman

Publisher's Cataloging-in-Publication Data

Miech, Irina.
  Irina's inspirations for jewelry : from the exotic to the everyday / Irina Miech.

    p. : col. ill. ; cm.

  ISBN: 978-0-87116-402-5

    1. Jewelry making. 2. Wire jewelry. 3. Wire jewelry—Patterns. 4. Beadwork.
    5. Beadwork—Patterns. I. Title.

TT212 .M5434 2011
739.27

Contents

Introduction   6

Materials & Design   8

Tools & Techniques   12

Projects

Changing Leaves   16
necklace

Water Lily   20
necklace

Beach Stones   23
necklace & earrings

Nature's Painting   26
necklace

Sepia Tones   30
necklace & earrings

Here Comes the Bride   34
necklace & earrings

Glass Sculpture   38
necklace set

Elizabethan Pearls   42
necklace set & earrings

Shades of the Ocean   46
necklace

Starry Night   50
necklace

Vibrant Reef   53
necklace

Personal Adornment   56
necklace & earrings

Fantasy Pod   60
necklace

Hawaiian Isles   64
bracelet

Victorian Cameo   68
necklace

Splendor   72
bracelet & earrings

Calla Lily   76
necklace

Globetrotter   80
necklace

Twisting Vine   84
bracelet

Botanical Tiles   88
bracelet

Gerbera Daisy   92
pendant

Nouveau Elegance   98
necklace & earrings

Timeless Gears   102
bracelet

Tree of Life   106
necklace

Acknowledgments   111

Introduction

Recognizing inspiration

Inspiration is a key component of creativity. Inspiration can come from nearly anywhere—the colors of a sunset, the shape of a stone, the texture of a flower's petals. Every time you notice these details, every time you're drawn to a leaf, every time you hear a piece of music that moves you, every time you hear a story or read a book that you keep going back to in your mind…that is inspiration. As jewelry makers, inspiration can bring us amazing treasures if we know how to recognize it—and it's always there, waiting to be tapped, even when we're not aware of it.

We surround ourselves with what inspires us; these are the things that spark our creativity and make us happy. Whether you're buying clothes, home furnishings, or flowers for your garden, you are buying things that inspire you. Learning to observe allows us to tap into these moments of creativity. You don't have to go far to find these sources of inspiration; look at the choices you have made in decorating, in planting gardens, and in your clothes closet. You'll discover colors and motifs that are significant and meaningful to you.

This book is a reflection of my own home and my life, and within the photos and jewelry projects you can see many of the things that inspire me. Around my house are many nature-inspired things: organically shaped candleholders, bowls that look like leaves, tiles with tree designs, and many, many more. My walls are covered with photos and paintings from my travels, I have lamps that look like trees, and the design of my tables reflects an Art Nouveau influence. These items are beautiful to me and I find them personally inspiring.

I chose many of these pieces, and some were given to me as gifts. We choose objects that appeal to us, that we connect with on a personal level. Things that are given to us often have a sentimental attachment, and the items we gather on our journeys often become a part of us and influence us, sparking moments of creativity.

As I was designing projects for this book, I began to focus on what inspired me, and I started noticing other forms of inspiration nearby. I saw patterns emerging as I realized that many of my earlier pieces had elements in common with the art I've surrounded myself with in my home. For my book *Beautiful Wire Jewelry for Beaders 2*, for example, I designed a ring called Copper Moon. Hanging in my foyer is a photograph called Moonrise. I did not notice the connection between the two until I started writing this book. It was interesting to look at the objects in my home and see how many common threads they share with my designs from previous books.

Not every inspiration is meant to come to fruition as a piece of jewelry. But if you start paying attention to these inspirations, you will find yourself on a creative artistic journey. We carry these pieces of inspiration in our minds everywhere we go, and when we see that special component or the perfect bead color that resonates, inspired design can start to take shape.

Irina Miech

We'll start out easy...

I structured the order of the projects in this book so you would find the least-complicated projects in the beginning to help you learn and master techniques such as making wire loops. Each fundamental skill is detailed in the first project that uses it. (If you need a review, turn to the summary of these techniques that starts on p. 13.) As you move through the book, the projects get a little more challenging. After the first few projects, I assume that you've learned the steps for the fundamental skills, so I don't repeat them every time.

Choosing materials

While gathering materials for each project, you can easily make substitutions in your choice of metal for wire, jump rings, and findings. I list the material I used to make the project as shown, but you can usually substitute your favorite metals or materials you have on hand.

Some people prefer to use a precious metal (sterling silver or gold-filled, for example) in their designs. Others choose less-expensive yet good-quality base metal alternatives, such as solid copper or plated copper in finishes such as gunmetal, a grayish color, or antique brass, a dark bronze color.

You can also make substitutions in sizes of components such as jump rings and beads. If you don't have the exact size listed, a close match will do.

If jump rings aren't specified as soldered, assume they are open. Regarding headpin length: If I don't specify a length in the materials list, the fairly common length of 1½" should work just fine.

Materials & Design

Material, shape, color, pattern, and other factors all come into play as you design beautiful jewelry. As you re-create projects in this book and begin designing your own pieces based on what inspires you, you'll learn how to control and adjust all the elements of good design.

Finding the right components

Today you'll find many choices in the bead marketplace that can help you bring an inspiration to life. As beaders, we often work with readymade components. Sometimes we can customize the components by altering elements, bending them, layering them, or by adding color. Unless we fabricate our own components from scratch, however, we often rely on a bit of serendipity in finding the components that correspond to our inspiration.

For example, it was good fortune to find the unusually shaped copper blanks as well as the flower and leaf components for the Botanical Tiles Bracelet—they allowed me to express my concept perfectly. Often when an inspiration is meaningful to me, whether it is a botanical element or an architectural detail, I do not set out to find components that remind me of it. The original inspiration remains with me in my subconscious. When I happen upon just the right component, I can begin my process.

Sometimes it's exactly the opposite. Sometimes a project starts with an idea, and I specifically search for components that reflect it. For example, for the Fantasy Pod project, I knew I wanted to create a necklace, but I didn't start with a specific component. Instead I looked for components that reminded me of the pod shape and its various parts. I searched through a variety of pieces, auditioning elements by placing them together, and the design started coming together through the process of experimentation and elimination until I found just the right combination.

Another example is the Water Lily project. I've loved Monet's water lily paintings for many years, and naturally they provided great inspiration for a project. I wanted a central component to express the inspiration and was happy to find a silver charm that resembled a water lily.

Finding the right components is more than just matching pieces to the inspiration. It's also about remaining open to possibilities, even when you're not actively focused on the inspiration. You never know where you will find the perfect component you're looking for—or weren't looking for, as the case may be.

Choosing colors

One of the most important elements of jewelry design is color. Color can make a piece delightful or distracting. There are degrees of color gradation that you can incorporate in your pieces that will give your work a polished look. You can choose to create an impact with color, or create a soothing blend of colors.

I choose colors very carefully. A special aspect of beading is that beads can have varying degrees of translucency and opacity, which adds a new dimension of depth to consider. In the Shades of the Ocean project, you'll see how I have chosen colors to represent the natural inspiration and how the different colors, tones, and amount of translucence blend to create a harmonious whole. In this piece, I used transparent and very watery blues, subtly contrasted against bright aqua CZs and almost-opaque opalescent crystals. I added a neutral color, nearly colorless and somewhat transparent, to help ground the piece and give it a unified look. Often I choose colors that are next to each other on the color wheel, but I pay careful attention to tone—I include both bright and muted variations of the same color.

In the Vibrant Reef project (below), I incorporated a different colorway. I used a single color to keep the design together—in this case the amazonite beads—and used that to anchor the rest of the colors, including the purples and the yellows.

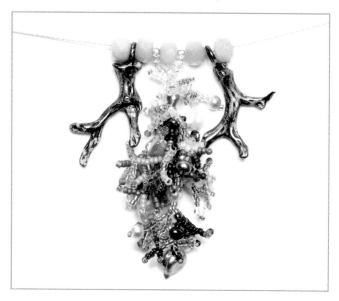

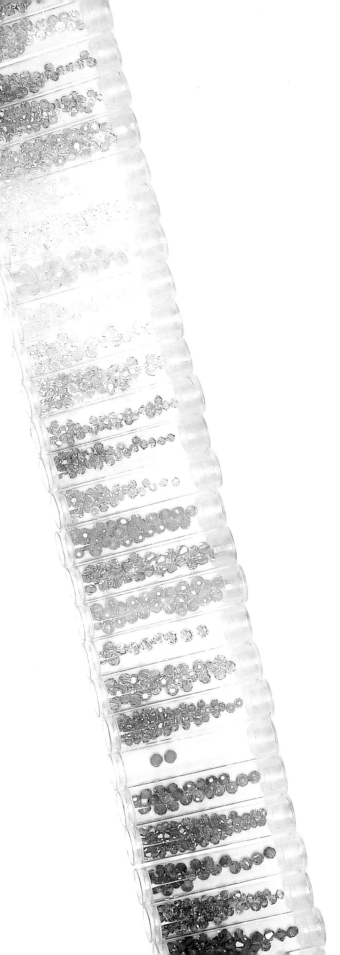

Achieving balance

Arranging patterns is a natural part of designing jewelry. Some pieces of jewelry are entirely about patterns and shapes, and contrasting them or combining them. Often, when people first start designing beaded jewelry, they tend to design very symmetrically— if you were to divide a necklace in half vertically, for example, one half would be a perfect mirror image of the other. There is a historical tradition of symmetrical jewelry dating back thousands of years. The eye is drawn to symmetry, and it seems ingrained in us to find it pleasing.

Another common element in jewelry design is the use of odd numbers of design elements, especially in necklaces. Designs that are pleasing to the eye often incorporate one, three, or five coordinating elements.

As you explore different styles, you sometimes discover the beauty of asymmetry. Finding out how to achieve a good asymmetrical design and balancing the whole look can be challenging. Even though the two sides of an asymmetrical design are not identical, it's most pleasing to the eye to have the same visual weight on both sides.

If, for example, you have a larger element on one side, then it's a good idea to have more small elements on the other side. Pattern is also very important. Even though you are designing asymmetrically, there will still be segments of pattern. These segments of pattern will also carry more visual weight than single elements, which will contribute to the overall balance. For example, the Elizabethan Pearls project (left) has three coordinating necklaces with a different asymmetrical pattern in each one.

Color also contributes to balance. If you are designing something that is not the same color on both sides, it still needs to have the same visual weight on both sides. If you use something bright on one side, it's a good idea to have something of the same intensity on the other side.

Watching trends

Trends often influence current jewelry designs. In this book, for example, I have several projects that incorporate metal. Fashion has embraced the look of metal, and we see this trend in the beading world as well.

For a long time, metal was seen simply as the setting or the hardware behind pretty beads, whether the beads were stone, glass, or pearls. Metal was a supporting element, something to construct clasps out of, or it was the chain that held the piece. Now metal is the focus of jewelry designs. Combining different metals is very popular and adds interest to the look of your jewelry. You can contrast metals in the same way that you do color. For example, you can use a silver rivet on a copper disk, as in the Tree of Life project. Or you can contrast copper and brass, as in the Botanical Tiles bracelet (below).

To add color and dimension to your metals, you can use a patina solution, such as liver of sulfur, or a wax-based colorant called Gilders Paste. In the Water Lily project, I used Gilders Paste to create a background for a bright silver pendant. In Vibrant Reef, I used color to blend the metal coral charms into the design.

Tools & Techniques

It's important to learn and practice different jewelry-making techniques so that you have a wide variety of tools in your toolkit—literally as well as figuratively speaking. Embrace and explore techniques that you've never tried before. Having a large variety of techniques at hand gives you tremendous versatility as you translate your inspiration into jewelry. The techniques you'll use to make the jewelry featured in this book range from simple stringing and crimping to wirework and easy metalworking.

Tools

Many tools, such as a set of jewelry pliers, you'll use again and again. Review the project you plan to make to be sure you have the tools needed—not every project uses every tool listed here.

Jewelry pliers and cutters
1 Chainnose pliers
2 Flatnose pliers
3 Roundnose pliers
4 Stepped roundnose pliers
5 Crimping pliers
6 Nylon-jaw pliers
7 Wire cutters

Metalworking tools
8 Steel bench block (with wooden dapping block)
9 Dead-blow hammer
10 Chasing hammer
11 Texturing hammer
12 Center punch
13 Metal stamps
14 Metal punch
15 Metal shears
16 Nylon-jaw bracelet forming pliers
17 Riveting hammer
18 Files

Additional tools and supplies (not shown)
• Beading needles and thread
• Bead Stoppers
• Chain Sta

Utility tools (handy for most projects, not shown)
• Ruler (inches and decimal)
• Fine-point permanent marker
• Pencil
• Scissors

Techniques summary

You'll need to know these basic beading and easy wireworking techniques for many of the projects in this book. Refer to this section if you need a quick lesson in any of these skills:

- **Crimping**
- **Working from the wire coil**
- **Making a basic loop**
- **Making a wrapped loop**

- **Opening/closing jump rings and basic loops**
- **Making a wire spiral**
- **Adding patina with liver of sulfur**

Crimping

To secure the ends of flexible beading wire, you'll need to use a crimping pliers and crimp beads. I use crimp beads that look like little tubes. Typically I'm using crimps to attach my clasps, but you will find other uses for them too.

To make a simple flat crimp, slide the crimp bead into place and squeeze it firmly with chainnose pliers.

For a more finished look, use crimping pliers: String a crimp bead on the beading wire **[a]**.

Pass the beading wire through the loop of the clasp (or other component) and back through the crimp bead **[b]**.

Grasp the crimp bead lightly in the back notches of the crimping pliers. Be sure the wires are separate and not overlapping in the bead, and close the jaws tightly on the bead. Each wire should be tightly enclosed in a channel created by the pliers **[c]**.

Move the bead so it is vertical in the front notches of the pliers **[d]**.

Close the jaws tightly so the bead folds in half, securing the beading wire **[e]**.

Trim the end of the beading wire close to where it exits the crimp bead **[f]**.

a

b

c

d

e

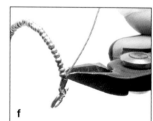

f

Working from the wire coil

If you work with wire often, you'll find it most economical as well as a real time-saver to work directly from the coil of wire as it comes from the package or spool. If you cut small lengths for each step, you'll need to trim the excess, thus accumulating a lot of short, wasted bits. Why not save time by eliminating several cutting and trimming steps?

Unless the project instructions specify a cut length for a step, assume you are working from the wire coil. If you are making basic or wrapped loops, place the bead on the wire first. If you forget and make a loop before you string the bead, you can string the bead on the other wire end before you make the final loop.

Some instructions call for forming loops above beads on headpins or eyepins. The process for making loops is very similar whether you are using a pin or working from the wire coil.

I am right-handed, and the photos show the actions as I do them. Most left-handers will need to use a mirror-image motion.

Making a basic loop above a bead

String a bead on a headpin. Make a right-angle bend over the bead **[a]**.

Grasp the wire with roundnose pliers just above the bend. Wrap the wire around the jaw as shown to form a circle **[b]**.

If necessary, reposition the pliers in the loop to continue wrapping the wire into a full loop. Trim the end to make a neat, full-circle loop **[c]**.

Use chainnose pliers to close the loop completely **[d]**.

To make loops on both sides of the bead, work from the wire coil and repeat the process on the opposite side. Make smaller loops by working toward the tip of the jaws.

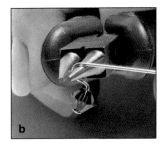

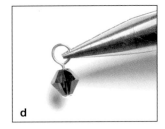

Making a wrapped loop

Begin the loop:
String a bead on a headpin or the wire coil. Grasp the wire with the tip of the chainnose pliers just above the bead if on a headpin (1¼" from the end if on the wire coil) and use your fingers to bend the wire over the pliers at a 90-degree angle **[a]**.

Place the roundnose pliers just past the bend. Wrap the wire over the top jaw as far as it will go **[b]**.

Rotate the pliers in the loop and continue wrapping until you have a full circle **[c]**.

If necessary, center the loop over the bead by turning the pliers slightly while holding the bead. When the loop is centered, the wire should cross itself at a 90-degree angle. At this point, the loop is open and you can connect it to another component, such as chain **[d]**.

Finish the loop:
Holding the loop with chainnose pliers, use your fingers or a second set of pliers to wrap the wire into the gap between the loop and the bead. Make 2–3 wraps **[e]**.

Trim the wire end close to the wraps **[f]**.

Use chainnose pliers to tuck the wire end tightly between the wraps and the bead **[g]**.

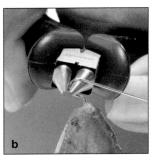

Opening jump rings and basic loops

To open: Using two sets of pliers, grasp one end of the ring in the tip of each pliers. Move one set of pliers toward you and one away to open the ring slightly.

To close: Reverse the motion. Use the same method to open a basic loop, add components, and close the loop.

Adding patina with liver of sulfur

A liver of sulfur (LOS) solution will darken sterling or fine silver and copper to give it an antiqued look. Dissolve dry chunks in a small bowl of warm water and dip the piece using tweezers or wire. Use a cotton swab to apply LOS gel full strength or slightly diluted. When you see a patina you like, stop the reaction by rinsing the piece in cold water. Dry the piece and brush with a polishing pad or super-fine steel wool to reveal some highlights.

Making a wire spiral

Working at the tip of the roundnose pliers, make a tiny loop at the end of a wire **[a]**.

Trim the tip of the loop if it's not curved **[b]**.

Continue shaping the wire with roundnose pliers to make a second loop around the first **[c]**.

Grasp the spiral with flatnose pliers and guide the wire with your fingers to continue shaping the spiral. Loosen the grip, reposition and regrip the spiral, and continue shaping until the spiral is the size you like **[d]**.

These photos show a loose spiral; you can shape a tighter spiral by using smaller, more controlled movements.

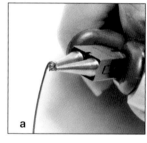

a

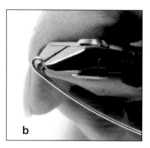

b

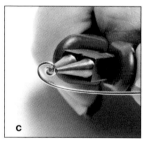

c

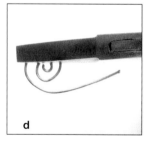

d

Changing Leaves
necklace

materials
- 7 16–28mm metal leaves
- 28–30 4mm–6mm bicone and round crystals
- 12–15" 22-gauge wire
- 24" chain
- 13 headpins
- 21 jump rings
- Hook clasp
- 2" chain for extender

tools
- Roundnose pliers
- Chainnose pliers
- Flatnose pliers
- Wire cutters
- Chain Sta chain holder

Fall is a truly amazing season in the Midwest. Although it's my favorite time of year, I also get nostalgic because the climate and flora of my adopted region are very similar to that of Kiev, where I was born. I think of it each year when the air turns crisp and cool and the colors begin to emerge.

The trees change to orange, purple, red, yellow … an explosion of colors everywhere I look. Some trees look like they're aflame. Sumac is especially vibrant, and maples look so full and brilliant. Birch trees turn a soft, glowing yellow. Some trees shed their leaves quickly, and some hold on to them far into the season. The varied shapes of their leaves intrigue me.

This necklace is inspired by all of these things—the beauty of fall, the way the leaves tumble in the wind, and the vibrancy of the colors all around. I chose Swarovski crystals in different colors and shapes, a variety of sterling silver leaves, and chain that continually moves and changes.

step 1

Cut the chain into two pieces: one 8" and one 16". As you create the necklace, you will cut random lengths (⅜–¾") of the 8" piece. Reserve the 16" piece for step 8.

step 2

String a crystal onto a headpin and make a basic loop. To make a loop, first make a right-angle bend over the bead.

step 3

Grasp the wire with roundnose pliers next to the bend. Wrap the wire around the jaw as shown to form a circle.

step 4

If necessary, reposition the pliers in the loop to continue wrapping the wire into a full loop. Trim the end to make a neat, full-circle loop.

step 5

Use two pairs of pliers (chainnose and flatnose) to open the loop slightly if needed. Connect the crystal dangle to one of the randomly sized chain pieces.

step 6

String a crystal onto the wire and make a loop at the end of the wire.

step 7

Make another loop over the crystal. Connect the bottom loop to the open end of the chain attached to the crystal dangle to make a chain-and-crystal component.

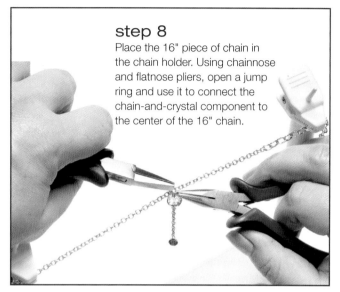

step 8

Place the 16" piece of chain in the chain holder. Using chainnose and flatnose pliers, open a jump ring and use it to connect the chain-and-crystal component to the center of the 16" chain.

Variation

Leaf charms are popular and fairly easy to find. Try a different metal finish with crystals for earrings.

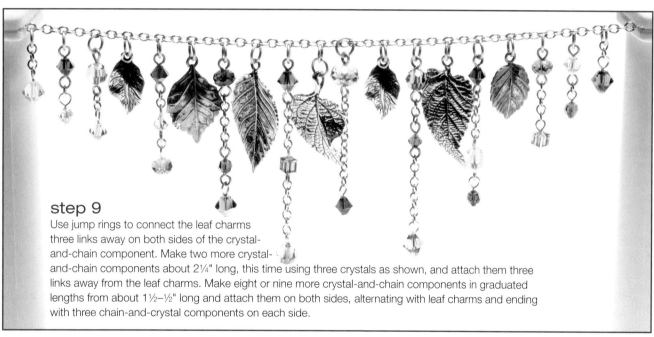

step 9

Use jump rings to connect the leaf charms three links away on both sides of the crystal-and-chain component. Make two more crystal-and-chain components about 2¼" long, this time using three crystals as shown, and attach them three links away from the leaf charms. Make eight or nine more crystal-and-chain components in graduated lengths from about 1½–½" long and attach them on both sides, alternating with leaf charms and ending with three chain-and-crystal components on each side.

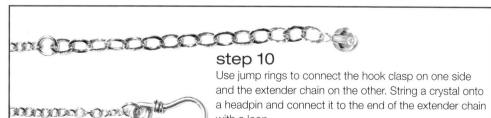

step 10

Use jump rings to connect the hook clasp on one side and the extender chain on the other. String a crystal onto a headpin and connect it to the end of the extender chain with a loop.

tip

The Chain Sta acts as an extra pair of hands as you attach components.

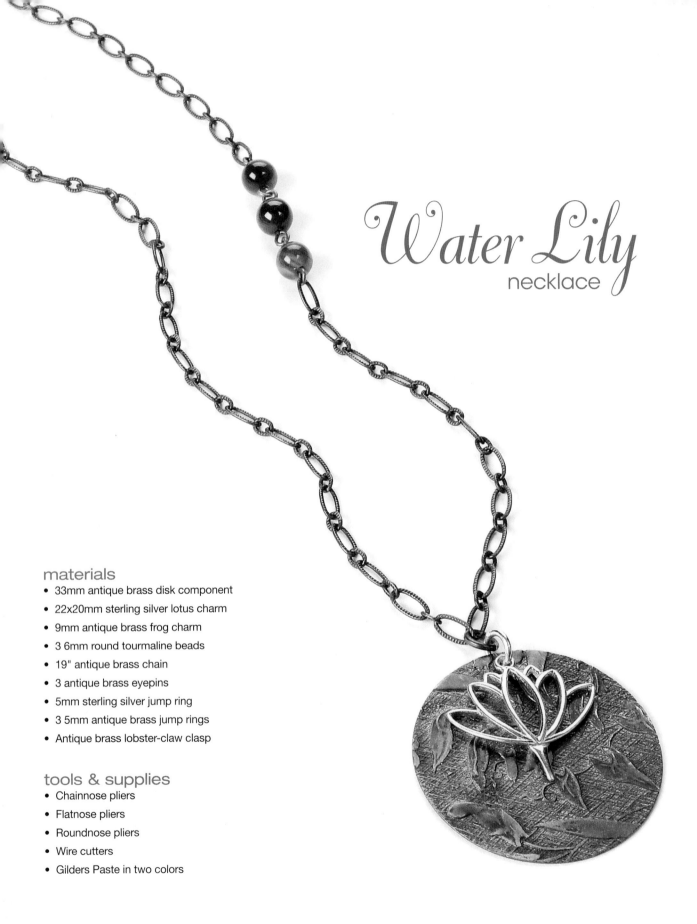

Water Lily
necklace

materials

- 33mm antique brass disk component
- 22x20mm sterling silver lotus charm
- 9mm antique brass frog charm
- 3 6mm round tourmaline beads
- 19" antique brass chain
- 3 antique brass eyepins
- 5mm sterling silver jump ring
- 3 5mm antique brass jump rings
- Antique brass lobster-claw clasp

tools & supplies

- Chainnose pliers
- Flatnose pliers
- Roundnose pliers
- Wire cutters
- Gilders Paste in two colors

Water Lilies

Sherrill

Water lilies remind me of vacationing with my parents as a child, as well as kayaking with my own children and sharing the beauty of nature with them. I love the serenity of water lilies and their resemblance to the lotus flower. In many cultures, this lovely flower is associated with enlightenment. To me, it signifies celebrating the beauty of nature in its purest form.

I'm always attracted to artwork that takes inspiration from these beautiful flowers, such as Monet's famous series of paintings. Several years ago, I met an artist named Sherrill Schoening who paints tropical designs on silk. I was immediately drawn to her paintings of water lilies, and I fell in love with Sherrill's style and the colors that she used. Today I enjoy the lush, nature-inspired look of three of her paintings in my home.

Sherrill's Water Lilies painting is a wonderful source of inspiration for jewelry. I chose a simple, stylized component that was a combination of water lily and lotus flower, echoing the simplicity of the single, half-opened lily. I layered the component over a background piece with a very subtle leaf pattern reminiscent of lily pads.

I wanted only a hint of color, and I also wanted to preserve the dark background of the antique brass. The lily in the painting is presented against the background of the lily pads and the dark and the light areas of the water. To reflect that, I used two different colors of Gilders Paste on the background component, a lighter color on the left and a darker on the right. The rest of the design is very simple: chain and three tourmaline beads on one side to reflect the colors of the painting.

This component from Lillypilly Designs is perfect for another interpretation of my inspiration.

Variation

step 1

Apply the Gilders Paste to the antique brass disk component with your finger using a light touch.

step 2

Use a sterling silver jump ring to connect the lotus charm to the antique brass disk component.

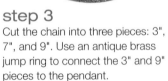

step 3

Cut the chain into three pieces: 3", 7", and 9". Use an antique brass jump ring to connect the 3" and 9" pieces to the pendant.

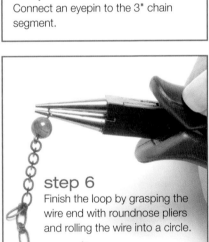

step 4

Connect an eyepin to the 3" chain segment.

step 6

Finish the loop by grasping the wire end with roundnose pliers and rolling the wire into a circle.

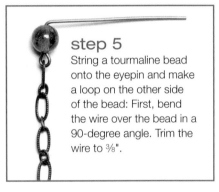

step 5

String a tourmaline bead onto the eyepin and make a loop on the other side of the bead: First, bend the wire over the bead in a 90-degree angle. Trim the wire to ⅜".

tip I used the paste colors called Patina and Iris Blue; colors can be blended. If you decide to try a different look, you can easily remove the paste with a wipe within half an hour of application.

step 7

Make two more gemstone components in the same way, connecting them as shown and adding the 7" chain segment to the last loop.

step 8

Connect the antique brass frog charm to the end of the 7" chain segment with a jump ring.

step 9

Attach a lobster-claw clasp to the 9" chain segment with a jump ring.

Beach Stones

necklace & earrings

materials

- Beach stone donut
- 9 large-hole beach stones
- 2 8–10mm matte-finish lampworked glass beads
- 3 5mm large-hole matte-finish semi-precious stone beads
- 7 4mm large-hole semiprecious stone bead rondelles
- 8–10" small-link sterling silver cable chain
- 7 10mm sterling silver jump rings
- 15 8mm textured jump rings
- 29 5mm sterling silver jump rings
- Sterling silver hook clasp
- Pair of sterling silver earring wires

tools

- Chainnose pliers
- Flatnose pliers
- Wire cutters

The surfaces of beach stones show the passage of time. The stones are held in the waves, rolling back and forth, slowly refined over many, many years into smooth shapes that are a delight to touch and hold.

Beach stones are irresistible to me. I always want to pick them up and fill my pockets with them. They glisten in the water; when dry, they have a beautiful subtle color and matte finish. Handling them later in my studio always reminds me of being on the beach and swimming in the ocean.

The drilled stones in this jewelry set came from my friend Tony Shafton, who collects and drills stones found on the shores of Lake Michigan. Because beach stones have such subtle colors, I chose other matte-finish beads with large holes to complement them as well as beads by lampwork artist Jeff Plath. I wanted to keep the focus on the beautiful beach stones, so the balance of the design is simple—just chain and jump rings— some smooth and some textured. The textured jump rings reflect the organic nature of the stones.

necklace, step 1

Cut the chain into 14 pieces of various sizes between ⅝–¾". Use a 5mm jump ring to attach a hook clasp to a short piece of chain.

step 2

String 1–3 beach stones and beads on the chain and connect the end link of chain to a textured jump ring with a plain jump ring. Use another plain jump ring to connect to the next length of chain, string beads, and add jump rings in the same way to the end link. Continue adding beaded segments, varying the number of beads per segment and contrasting the shapes and colors on each subsequent piece of chain.

step 3

Use 10mm plain jump rings to connect beach stone donuts between the textured jump rings.

step 4

When you reach the desired length, finish by connecting a final beach stone to the necklace with a large plain jump ring. Any of the textured jump rings can be used as the loop of the clasp.

earrings, step 1

Cut two ⅝" pieces of chain. Attach a large jump ring to a beach stone. Connect the large jump ring to one piece of chain with a small jump ring.

step 2

String a small stone on the chain and connect an earring wire to the other end of the chain. Make a second earring.

I used Gilders Paste to add a mist of color to this beach stone.

Variation

Nature's Painting
necklace

materials
- Semiprecious stone focal pendant
- Assorted semiprecious stone beads (about 12, ranging from 10–30mm)
- 25–30 3mm gemstone rondelles
- 40–45 2mm fine silver beads
- Flexible beading wire, .019
- 24-gauge sterling silver headpin
- Sterling silver crimp beads
- Sterling silver hook
- 6" large-link sterling silver chain for extender

tools
- Chainnose pliers
- Roundnose pliers
- Wire cutters
- Crimping pliers

tip I suggest you keep a second wire cutters to use only on beading wire. This wire has a steel core that can ruin cutters you use on softer metals such as sterling silver.

Nature creates masterpieces. Everywhere you look, there is something amazing: forests, mountains, clouds, rock—all of these elements possess a striking appearance that you can draw from for your own designs.

While we were kayaking in the Wisconsin Dells, incredible works of nature's art presented themselves around every bend of the river: the eroded rock, with its artistic shapes and layers of color, and the beautiful trees. This is one of the most picturesque places on earth.

For this necklace, I chose as my centerpiece a framed gemstone that reminds me of both the river and the landscape with its many layers of color. I chose the other elements to reflect the shapes and colors of the rocks, the trees, and the sky. I strung random patterns of beads on each side of the pendant to reflect the way that nature serendipitously arranges her artwork.

TONY MIECH

step 1

Center the pendant on a piece of beading wire. Add assorted semiprecious beads and rondelles spaced with 2mm fine silver beads until you reach the desired length (my necklace is 13" without the chain extenders).

step 2

Cut the chain into two pieces: 1½" and 4¼". Crimp the short piece of chain to one end of the beaded strand and attach the hook to the end link of chain.

step 3

Crimp the longer piece of chain to the other end of the strand.

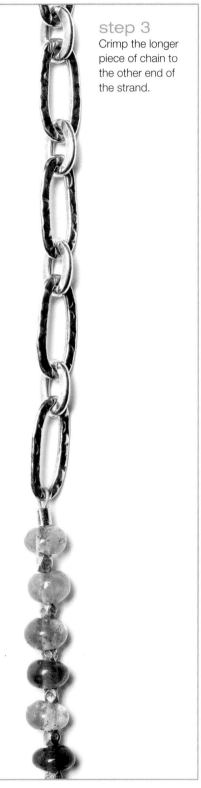

Variation

I knotted gorgeous jasper and other gemstone beads onto silk thread for this variation on the Nature's Painting theme.

step 4—make a wrapped-loop dangle

For the dangle at the end of the longer chain, string a semiprecious stone bead onto a headpin and attach it to the last chain link with a wrapped loop.

To make a wrapped loop, first grasp the wire directly over the bead with the tip of the chainnose pliers and make a 90-degree bend in the wire over the pliers **[a]**.

Place the roundnose pliers just past the bend and wrap the wire over the top jaw **[b]**.

Continue wrapping the wire as far as it will go **[c]**. Rotate the pliers in the loop slightly and continue wrapping until you have a full circle **[d]**.

If necessary, center the loop over the bead by turning the pliers slightly while holding the bead. When the loop is centered, the wire should cross itself at a 90-degree angle **[e]**.

Connect the loop to the last chain link. Holding the loop with chainnose pliers, use your fingers or a second set of pliers to wrap the wire into the gap between the loop and the bead. Make 2–3 wraps **[f]**.

Trim the wire end close to the wraps **[g]**.

Use chainnose pliers to tuck the wire end tightly between the wraps and the bead **[h]**.

The completed dangle at the end of the extender chain **[i]**.

a

b

c

d

e

f

g

h

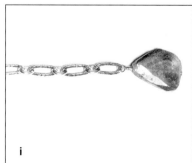

i

Sepia Tones

necklace
& earrings

I have always loved the design of the Art Nouveau period. The beautiful lines of the artwork, the amazing shapes of the architecture, and the rich detail of the jewelry are very inspiring.

Certain medallions, swirls, and intricate floral designs are very specific to this time period, and you see them again and again—in furniture design, architecture, fabric and wallpaper patterns, and jewelry.

You'll discover that many jewelry components in the Art Nouveau style are available now; some are old pieces from the turn of the 20th century and some are reproductions made from original molds using the same processes, such as the components I used in this set. The tones of the antique brass pieces I used remind me of an old sepia-tone photograph.

materials

- 36x38mm antique-brass filigree component
- 24mm antique-brass goddess charm
- 2 20mm antique-brass Art Nouveau column components
- 8 8mm antique-brass flower charms
- 6 9mm antique-brass textured jump rings
- 36 4.5mm antique-brass jump rings
- 5 3mm antique-brass jump rings
- 29" antique-brass chain
- Lobster-claw clasp
- 2" large-link antique-brass chain for extender
- Pair of antique-brass earring wires

tools

- Chainnose pliers
- Flatnose pliers

necklace, step 1

Cut the antique brass chain into four pieces: two 7" pieces and two 7½" pieces. Connect the goddess charm to the large filigree component with a 3mm jump ring.

step 2

Connect a flower charm to the bottom of the large filigree component with a jump ring.

step 3

Connect the jump rings in the following pattern: pair of 4.5mm jump rings, 4.5mm jump ring, pair of 4.5mm jump rings, 9mm textured jump ring.

step 4

Repeat step 3 two times.

step 5

Connect the first pair of 4.5mm jump rings to the large filigree component.

step 6

Connect a flower charm to each textured ring with a 4.5mm jump ring.

step 7

Connect two pieces of chain to the end textured jump ring, placing the 7" piece on top and the 7½" piece on the bottom.

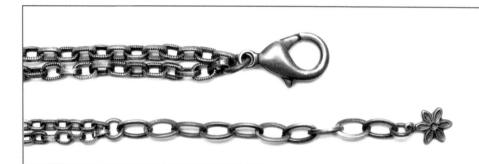

step 8

Repeat steps 3–7 for the other side of the necklace. One one end, use jump rings to attach the clasp. On the other end, use a jump ring to attach the extender chain. Attach a flower charm to the end with a jump ring.

■ earrings, step 1

Use 3mm jump rings to connect the flower charms to the column component.

step 2

Use a 4.5mm jump ring to connect the earring to the earring wire. Make a second earring.

Variation

The filigree component nestles around a topaz-colored vintage glass cabochon in this Sepia Tones ring.

Here Comes
the Bride
necklace & earrings

The ceremony that unites two people in matrimony is a momentous occasion, and the joyful celebration that follows brings families and friends together as well. For many people, a wedding is one of the most important days of their lives.

Since Victorian times, brides in many cultures have traditionally worn a white wedding dress. Often made of elegant fabric and elaborately adorned, the wedding gown has become an symbol of the wedding day and the celebration of marriage. Echoing the elegant look of the gown, bridal jewelry has its own traditions and usually includes pearls, crystals, or diamonds.

This is a picture of my dear friend's mother, Clara Matusko, on her wedding day in 1939. The dress, the flowers, the backdrop—all capture a time when weddings had a grandeur that's different than the ceremonies of modern times.

For this project, I wanted to create a timeless look that transcends trends—jewelry that would look appropriate worn today or 100 years ago. The half-drilled pearls are timeless. The other components are contemporary, but they take their inspiration from jewelry designs of the past.

materials
- Focal filigree-and-crystal component
- 3 11mm half-drilled pearls
- 16 3mm crystal pearls
- 8 4mm crystal spacers
- 3 post bead cap components
- 16–18" 24-gauge half-hard sterling silver wire
- 14–16" fine-cable sterling silver chain
- 5mm soldered sterling silver jump ring
- 3mm sterling silver jump ring
- Clasp
- Pair of post earring components

tools & supplies
- Chainnose pliers
- Roundnose pliers
- Wire cutters
- Two-part epoxy

necklace, step 1

Use two-part epoxy to adhere the pearl to the post bead cap component.

step 2

Attach the pearl drop to the loop at the bottom of the focal component.

step 3

Cut six three-link pieces of chain.

step 4

Start a wrapped-loop component using a pearl, a spacer, and a pearl, making the loops small so they are in proportion to the chain links. Don't wrap the loops yet.

step 5

Slip a three-link chain segment into each loop and finish the wrapped loops.

step 6

Continue this pattern until you have three chain segments and three wrapped-loop components. Don't wrap the last loop of the last component yet.

step 7

Attach a long piece of chain to the last loop and wrap the loop.

step 8

Repeat steps 4–7 to make a second section of chain with wrapped-loop components.

step 9

Open the top loops of the focal component and connect one to each of the chain sections.

step 10

Attach the clasp by opening a connector loop on the clasp. Attach the soldered jump ring using an open 3mm jump ring.

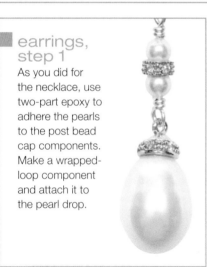

earrings, step 1

As you did for the necklace, use two-part epoxy to adhere the pearls to the post bead cap components. Make a wrapped-loop component and attach it to the pearl drop.

step 2

Attach the post earring component to the wrapped-loop component by opening the connector loop.

Variation

Pay close attention to the details! You'll discover wonderful components that add up to create the look you're after.

Glass Sculpture
necklace set

materials

- 20x14mm riveted lampworked focal bead
- 35 garnet briolettes, graduated in size from 6–10mm long
- 126–130 3mm faceted garnet beads
- 126–130 2mm Hill Tribes silver spacer beads
- 280–300 2mm Hill Tribes silver cube beads
- Flexible beading wire
- 38" garnet beaded chain
- 24-gauge sterling silver headpin
- 2 10mm sterling silver textured jump rings
- 4 4mm sterling silver jump rings
- 6 sterling silver crimp beads
- 6 sterling silver spring rings
- Sterling silver hook clasp
- 2" sterling silver chain for extender

tools

- Chainnose pliers
- Flatnose pliers
- Roundnose pliers
- Wire cutters
- Crimping pliers

KRISTINA RENEE

Many years ago a friend showed me how to make beads by melting glass onto a steel mandrel over a torch flame. Having experienced this lampworking process, which is sometimes called flameworking, makes me appreciate how much skill, creativity, and precision goes into each of these miniature works of art. Every strand of glass, every dot, and every speck of color is added by hand with great purpose, creating a beautiful glass sculpture in miniature.

The color and simplicity of this glass bead by artist Tammy Rae Wolter (above) appealed to me, and I like the texture and spark of color the silver rivets add. When selecting materials to complement this beautiful focal bead, I purposely chose not to imitate every color of the bead, but rather committed to one color and used that color in a variety of shades as a strong background. This color choice relates to the focal bead without overpowering it. This is the heart of the project: selecting components to complement the focal bead. I used Hill Tribes silver accents to reflect the texture of the rivets.

I constructed this necklace so that it could be worn in several different ways. Each strand ends in a spring ring, which independently clips onto large jump rings that are attached to the clasp. This way any combination of strands can be worn. I also added an extender chain that allows for more possibilities and varying lengths.

39

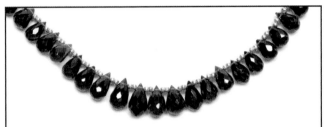

shortest (16") strand, step 1

Cut a 20" piece of flexible beading wire and string the garnet briolettes, keeping them in graduated order and alternating with 2mm Hill Tribes silver spacer beads.

step 2

When you run out of briolettes, string 2mm Hill Tribes spacers until you reach 16".

step 3—crimping

Crimp a spring-ring clasp to each end of the beading wire.

To crimp, first string a crimp bead on the wire [a]. Pass the beading wire through the loop of a spring-ring clasp and back through the crimp bead [b].

Grasp the crimp bead lightly in the back notches of the crimping pliers. Be sure the wires are separate and not overlapping in the bead, and close the jaws tightly on the bead [c]. Each wire should be tightly enclosed in a channel created by the pliers.

Move the bead so it is vertical in the front notches of the pliers.

Close the jaws tightly so the bead folds in half, tightly securing the beading wire [d, e]. Trim the end of the beading wire close to where it exits the crimp bead [f].

The finished crimp [g].

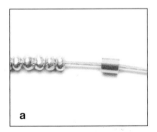

a

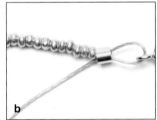

b

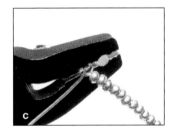

c

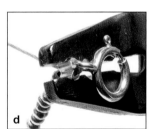

d

e

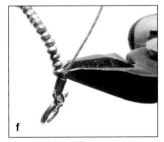

f

g

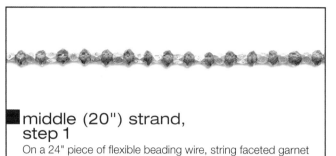

middle (20") strand, step 1

On a 24" piece of flexible beading wire, string faceted garnet beads alternating with Hill Tribes silver cube beads until you reach nearly 10".

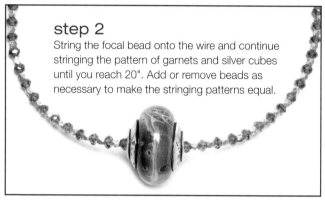

step 2

String the focal bead onto the wire and continue stringing the pattern of garnets and silver cubes until you reach 20". Add or remove beads as necessary to make the stringing patterns equal.

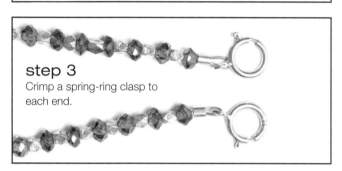

step 3

Crimp a spring-ring clasp to each end.

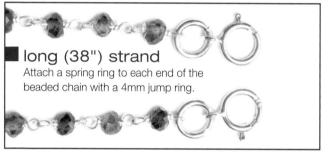

long (38") strand

Attach a spring ring to each end of the beaded chain with a 4mm jump ring.

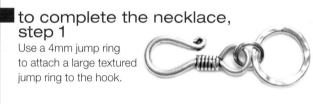

to complete the necklace, step 1

Use a 4mm jump ring to attach a large textured jump ring to the hook.

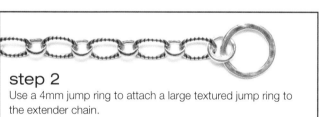

step 2

Use a 4mm jump ring to attach a large textured jump ring to the extender chain.

step 3

String a faceted garnet bead and a Hill Tribes cube onto the headpin and attach it to the end of the extender chain with a wrapped loop.

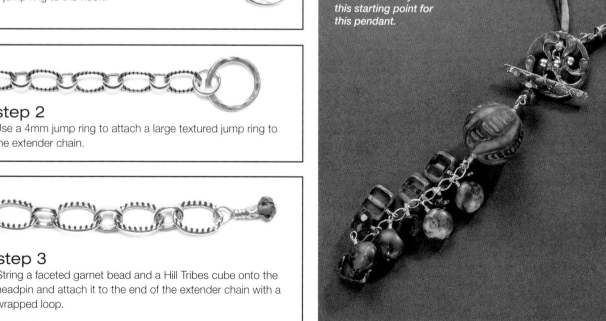

Variation

An art bead by Harold Williams Cooney was this starting point for this pendant.

Elizabethan Pearls
necklace set & earrings

The Elizabethan era is known as a time of exquisite clothing and jewelry. Fabrics of the nobility were rich and sumptuous: thick brocades, expensive linen with embroidery and lace details, and vibrant, jewel-colored hues. Clothing was embellished with gemstones and pearls, and embroidery glistened with gold and silver threads.

In this iconic portrait of Queen Elizabeth by George Gowan, her dress is heavily embellished with pearls, large teardrop-shaped pearls adorn the front of her dress, and she wears pearl necklaces, pearl earrings, and pearls in her hair.

For my necklace based on this painting, I used cultured freshwater baroque pearls as the focal points because of their interesting shapes. (The term "baroque" refers to the irregular shape of the pearls.) I carefully arranged the pearls so they graduate in size. The ball headpins and the long wrap I used are patterned after the teardrop pearls in the portrait.

I also chose three complementary colors of Swarovski pearls to reflect the look of the inspiration. The dark strand adds dimension. The antique brass bead caps suggest the lace of the time period, and rich crystals add luxurious colors.

Versatile jewelry that can be worn in different ways probably wasn't a concern for Elizabeth, but it fits today's lifestyles; these three strands can be worn together or separately. I also added some asymmetrical detail to make the look a bit more contemporary.

materials

Teardrop necklace, 18" plus extender

- 7 18–20mm baroque pearls
- 70–80 6mm Swarovski pearls
- 34 gold-tone bead caps
- Flexible beading wire, .014 (cut to 20")
- 8 gold-filled ball headpins
- 2 gold-tone crimp beads
- Gold-tone hook clasp
- 2" gold-tone large-link chain for extender

White pearl necklace, 48"

- 104 8mm Swarovski pearls
- 7 8mm crystal rounds
- 14 6mm rhinestone rondelles
- Flexible beading wire, .014 (cut to 50")
- 5mm gold-tone jump ring
- 2 gold-tone crimp beads or tubes
- Gold-tone lobster-claw clasp

Champagne pearl necklace, 51"

- 113 8mm Swarovski pearls
- 16 antique brass bead caps
- Flexible beading wire, .014 (cut to 53")
- 5mm antique brass jump ring
- 2 brass crimp beads
- Antique brass lobster-claw clasp

Silver-gray pearl necklace, 54"

- 111 8mm Swarovski pearls
- 6 8mm rhinestone filigree beads
- 16 6mm crystal rounds
- 8 6mm rhinestone rondelles
- Flexible beading wire, .014 (cut to 56")
- 5mm gunmetal jump ring
- 2 gunmetal crimp beads
- Gunmetal lobster-claw clasp

Teardrop earrings

- 2 18–20mm baroque pearls
- 2 6mm Swarovski pearls
- 4 gold-tone bead caps
- 2 gold-filled ball headpins
- 5–6" 24-gauge gold-filled wire
- Pair of earring wires

tools

- Chainnose pliers
- Roundnose pliers
- Wire cutters
- Crimping pliers

teardrop necklace, step 1

To make the pearl-and-headpin components, first string a large teardrop-shaped pearl on a ball headpin.

step 2

With chainnose or flatnose pliers, make a right-angle bend in the wire approximately 3–4mm above the pearl.

step 3

Use roundnose pliers to make a loop. Wrap the end of the wire in a long coil below the loop and trim the excess wire. Tuck the tail in with chainnose pliers. Using pearls of different sizes, repeat steps 1–3 to create six more pearl dangles.

step 4

Center the largest pearl dangle in the center of a 20" piece of flexible beading wire. On each end, string a bead cap, three 6mm pearls, and another bead cap.

step 5

Continue to string this pattern, graduating the sizes of the pearl dangles until you've used all of them. End with a bead cap.

step 6

String this pattern on both ends: three 6mm pearls, a bead cap, a pearl, and a bead cap. Continue the pattern until you reach the desired length, ending with a pearl.

step 7

Crimp a hook clasp to one end.

step 8

Crimp the extender chain to the other end. String a 6mm pearl on a ball headpin and attach it to the end link of the chain with a wrapped loop.

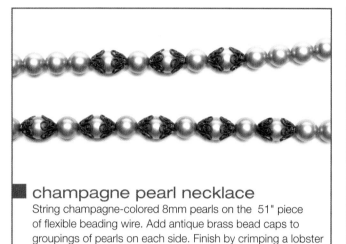

champagne pearl necklace

String champagne-colored 8mm pearls on the 51" piece of flexible beading wire. Add antique brass bead caps to groupings of pearls on each side. Finish by crimping a lobster claw and soldered jump ring to the ends.

white pearl necklace

step 1

String white 8mm pearls on the 48" piece of flexible beading wire. Add groupings of crystal gold-tone rondelles and round crystal beads on one side of the necklace.

step 2

Finish by crimping a lobster-claw clasp and a soldered jump ring to the ends.

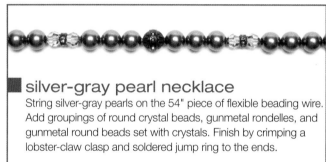

silver-gray pearl necklace

String silver-gray pearls on the 54" piece of flexible beading wire. Add groupings of round crystal beads, gunmetal rondelles, and gunmetal round beads set with crystals. Finish by crimping a lobster-claw clasp and soldered jump ring to the ends.

earrings

String a teardrop-shaped pearl on a ball headpin. Make a wrapped loop with 3–4mm of coil between the loop and the pearl. Using gold-filled wire, make another wrapped loop and attach the pearl dangle. String a bead cap, a 6mm pearl, and a bead cap. Begin a wrapped loop at the other end. String an earwire on the loop and finish wrapping the loop. Make another earring.

Variation

Hand-carved smoky topaz beads reflect an Elizabethan aesthetic.

Shades of the Ocean
necklace

Being on an oceanfront is one of my favorite ways to spend a vacation. I've seen the ocean from many different beaches, and it has many moods. Sometimes it's green, sometimes sky blue, sometimes dark. Sometimes you see all of its colors at once.

I love the ocean best in Tahiti. It is a splendid, vibrant blue, and the blue grows deeper and deeper the farther you look. The water is so clear and you can see very far into its depths. It's warm and inviting, welcoming me to jump in.

This project is about the shifting boundary between ocean and land. Beach gives way to ocean, transitioning from sand to sea. There is an ever-changing line of sea foam at the edge, where the warm color of the sand gives way to the different shades of blue. Farther out, one can see the reflection of sun on water, where the sea shimmers and sparkles in a magical way.

I used vacation photos to guide me as I selected the colors for this necklace, which mirror the transition from sand to foam to ocean to deep blue. To show the sparkle of sun on water, I used silver charlottes. I used different shades of Swarovski crystals and CZs, including opal colors and muted hues to give the necklace depth. I used small beads knowing I would have the visual weight of multiple strands, and I varied the shapes to create further interest.

materials
- 600–650 2–4mm crystal bicones, rounds, and CZ beads in many shades of blue and tan
- 20 grams 11° silver-finish charlottes
- 2 sterling silver jump rings
- 2 sterling silver cones
- 6" 22-gauge sterling silver half-hard wire
- Flexible beading wire, .014
- 3 sterling silver headpins
- 14 sterling silver crimp tubes
- Sterling silver hook clasp
- 2" sterling silver chain for extender

tools
- Bead Stoppers (large)
- Chainnose pliers
- Roundnose pliers
- Wire cutters
- Crimping pliers

TONY MIECH

tip

A charlotte is a glass seed bead with a single facet, which gives these beads brilliant sparkle. Charlottes are available in many colors, including metal finishes such as silver and gold. Metal-coated charlottes are a bit heavier than glass charlottes, and they are often sold on short hanks or in smaller quantities.

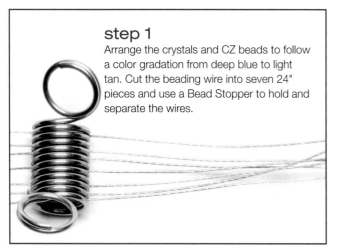

step 1

Arrange the crystals and CZ beads to follow a color gradation from deep blue to light tan. Cut the beading wire into seven 24" pieces and use a Bead Stopper to hold and separate the wires.

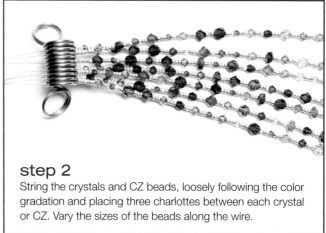

step 2

String the crystals and CZ beads, loosely following the color gradation and placing three charlottes between each crystal or CZ. Vary the sizes of the beads along the wire.

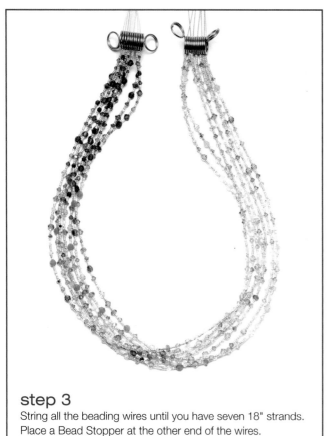

step 3

String all the beading wires until you have seven 18" strands. Place a Bead Stopper at the other end of the wires.

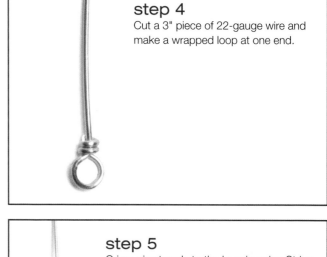

step 4

Cut a 3" piece of 22-gauge wire and make a wrapped loop at one end.

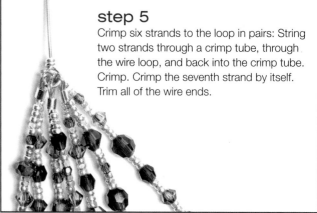

step 5

Crimp six strands to the loop in pairs: String two strands through a crimp tube, through the wire loop, and back into the crimp tube. Crimp. Crimp the seventh strand by itself. Trim all of the wire ends.

step 6
String the wire through the cone.

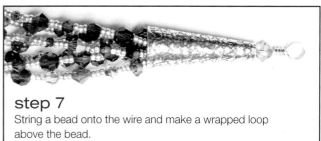

step 7
String a bead onto the wire and make a wrapped loop above the bead.

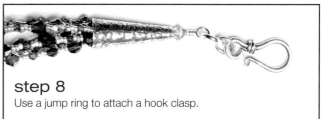

step 8
Use a jump ring to attach a hook clasp.

Variation

The two-hole crystals, backed by silver foil, remind me of the way the ocean reflects sunlight. I added other shades of blue-green and mixed finishes as well.

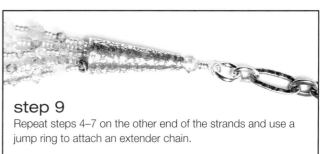

step 9
Repeat steps 4–7 on the other end of the strands and use a jump ring to attach an extender chain.

step 10
String three crystals onto headpins and attach them to the last link of the extender chain with wrapped loops.

Starry Night
necklace

materials

- 1" (25mm) borosilicate glass focal pendant
- 40–50 4–12mm crystal beads, assorted shapes and colors
- 20–24" fine-link gunmetal cable chain
- Gunmetal ball headpin
- 40–48 22-gauge gunmetal eyepins
- 3 oval gunmetal jump rings
- Gunmetal lobster-claw clasp
- 12–16" large-link gunmetal cable chain for extender

tools

- Chainnose pliers
- Flatnose pliers
- Roundnose pliers
- Wire cutters

The night sky has held the imagination of countless civilizations, inspiring legends, mythology, and worship. Its vast depths have always been a source of wonder. Bright stars and spiraling galaxies are scattered across the black canvas of the night, creating patterns that were fertile sources for the Greeks, who created an entire pantheon of beings from the images they saw in these stars.

I love being outside at night in any remote area. With few lights to compete, the night sky offers up some incredible sights.

When I first saw Keith Kreitter's borosilicate glass pendants, they immediately reminded me of spiraling galaxies, nebulas, and star clusters—beautiful and mysterious places in the universe. Each pendant is its own little self-contained magical galaxy. With the pendant in hand, I began to select colors of crystal, drawing from the pendant itself as well as the inspirational photo. To mirror the color of the night sky, I used gunmetal-color chain and findings.

The finished piece surprised me. The colors are not my normal palette, and I would not have chosen them had I not been working from this source of inspiration. That is the beauty of working with something so specific: It may inspire you to step away from preconceived outcomes or your favorite colors, and you will end up with something beautiful beyond your expectations.

NASA

step 1

Cut the fine- and the large-link chain into pieces of varying lengths from 1–2".

step 2

String the pendant onto a piece of fine-link chain. Connect an eyepin to one end of the chain.

step 3

String a crystal, make another loop above the crystal, and attach another piece of fine-link chain. Keep the pendant centered and continue to connect fine-link chain segments with eyepin-and-crystal components on both ends until you reach 8" in length.

step 4

Make two additional 8" lengths of chain and crystals using fine-link chain, and two 8" lengths using large-link chain. Gather the ends of the five chains in a jump ring. Gather the opposite ends in the same way.

step 5

Attach an eyepin to the jump ring, string a crystal, and make a loop above the crystal.

step 6

Continue to create and link eyepin-and-crystal components on each end until you reach the desired length.

step 7

Attach the lobster-claw clasp to one end with a jump ring.

step 8

Attach 2" of large-link cable chain to the other side as an extender. String a crystal onto a ball headpin, make a loop, and attach it to last link of the extender chain.

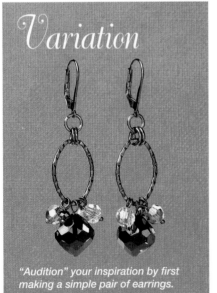

Variation

"Audition" your inspiration by first making a simple pair of earrings.

Vibrant Reef
necklace

materials

- 8 base metal coral charms
- 65–70 6mm amazonite rondelles
- 60–70 3–6mm pearls in various colors and shapes
- 80–120 2–3mm crystals
- 10 grams seed beads and cylinder beads in sizes ranging from 15º to 11º, assorted shapes and colors
- 20" flexible beading wire
- 24-gauge gunmetal headpin
- Two gunmetal crimp beads
- Gunmetal hook clasp
- 2" gunmetal chain for extender
- Fireline beading thread in Crystal

tools & supplies

- Gilders Paste in Patina
- Chainnose pliers
- Roundnose pliers
- Wire cutters
- Crimping pliers
- Scissors
- Beading needle

Fireline is a sturdy, braided thread. Designed as a sports fishing line, it's now readily available at bead stores and works great when you need a lightweight but tough thread.

MILA ZINKOVA

One of my favorite things to do is snorkel. It's amazing to be suspended in another world, one so different from our own, and to be rocked gently by the ocean as you swim in its warm embrace. It's almost like flying, in a way, because you can explore the three dimensions so fully.

When the ocean is completely clear, you can see such incredible things. The underwater world is vibrant and otherworldly, and it changes constantly, even in just the span of a few feet. Underneath the water are incredible gardens full of color and texture, with colorful little fish swimming in and out of them. Some corals look like flowers and others look like giant brains. They form entire landscapes that are gorgeous whether you're close-up or faraway. Hidden in this rich tapestry are amazing treasures, such as the beautiful giant clam in this photograph that is the color of the nearby coral. If you look closely, you'll see something mysterious and beautiful everywhere.

In my necklace design, I wanted to capture the color and texture of the reef—the essence of this photograph. I used an easy stitching technique to make branches that replicate the shapes and the texture of the coral. I used a variety of shapes and sizes of seed beads, pearls, and crystals to reflect the look of the coral and create a subtle, intuitive color gradation. I blended different colors such as the vibrant fuchsia from the photograph, using it at the bottom of the coral components, and adding patches of greens and sunny yellows. I stitched areas of brown that help blend the other colors. The great contrasting color of the baroque pearls are a natural fit for this project, and their irregular shapes add texture as well.

I also chose gunmetal coral charms to which I applied Gilders Paste. The color of the paste highlights the charms and makes them look like they're part of the reef. Placed between the stitched coral components, the charms add contrast, just as in the dark areas of the photo. I chose amazonite beads as my unifying color because they are the color of the water. They tie the entire design together.

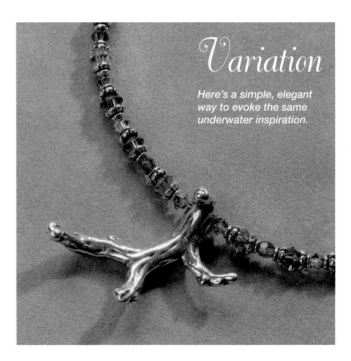

Variation

Here's a simple, elegant way to evoke the same underwater inspiration.

step 1

Apply the Gilders Paste to the coral charms with your finger. I used a single color called Patina to reflect the colors in my inspiration photo, but you can blend two or more colors if you wish.

step 2

To make the stitched coral components, thread a comfortable length of Fireline on your beading needle. Pick up four to six seed or cylinder beads and sew through an amazonite rondelle. Pick up another four to six beads, leaving a 4" tail. Tie the ends together with an overhand knot.

step 3

Pick up assorted sizes of beads and pearls in various colors until you reach the desired length of the "core" of the component. Pick up a pearl and a seed bead. Sew back through the seed bead and the pearl. Sew up through the core of beads to the point where you want to add a branch (two or three seed beads from the last pearl is a good place) and exit between the seed beads.

step 4

Pick up a few beads in a color similar to the beads you're exiting. After picking up the last bead, sew back through the seed beads in that branch until you reach the core. Sew back up the core until you reach the next place you want to place a branch. Repeat the branching technique as often as you like, adding pearls and crystals to some. Treat some of the branches as cores and create branches on those branches, always returning to the main core.

When you're pleased with the look of the branches, make a half-hitch knot anywhere along the core. Sew back through the core, sew back up or down a few beads, and trim the thread. Make nine stitched coral components in sizes graduating from about 1¼" to 2" long.

step 5

Cut a 24" piece of flexible beading wire. String the longest stitched coral component to the center of the flexible beading wire. One each side, string a 2mm crystal round, an amazonite rondelle, a coral charm, and an amazonite rondelle.

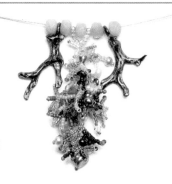

Continue to string in this pattern, alternating the stitched coral components with the coral charms and amazonite rondelles, and graduating the size of the stitched coral components until you have strung the smallest last. String amazonite rondelles alternating with seed beads on both sides until you reach the desired length.

step 6

Crimp the hook clasp to one end.

step 7

Crimp the extender chain to the other end. String an amazonite rondelle on a headpin, make a loop, and attach it to the last link of the extender chain.

how to tie a half-hitch knot

Pass the needle under the thread bridge between two beads, and pull gently until a loop forms. Cross back over the thread between the beads, sew through the loop, and pull gently to draw the knot into the beadwork.

Personal Adornment

necklace & earrings

materials

- 3 20mm faceted CZ drops
- 3 12mm faceted CZ drops
- 4mm faceted sodalite rondelles
- 20 Hill Tribes fine silver cube beads
- Sterling silver enhancer bail
- Flexible beading wire, .014
- 8–10" 24-gauge half-hard sterling silver wire
- 2" sterling silver fine-link cable chain
- 3 sterling silver cones
- 2 sterling silver crimp beads
- Sterling silver hook clasp
- 2" sterling silver chain for extender
- Pair of sterling silver earring wires

tools

- Chainnose pliers
- Flatnose pliers
- Roundnose pliers
- Wire cutters
- Crimping pliers

One of the best things about being a jewelry designer is that you can make the perfect accessory to complete any ensemble, whatever the occasion.

Sometimes the colors in a favorite outfit can turn out to be a great inspiration for jewelry that can be worn with many other pieces of clothing. The colors or features that attract us to that particular piece are often repeated in the rest of our wardrobe and tend to reflect our style. Even if your other clothing does not contain all of the same colors, the same piece of jewelry often will complement it.

As I created this piece, I kept in mind that even though I was making a piece of jewelry that would look good with my dress, I was also designing it to coordinate with other clothing in my wardrobe. To make it more versatile, I created a detachable focal pendant so I could simplify the necklace and wear it with other clothes.

necklace, step 1

Cut a 24" piece of flexible beading wire and string the faceted gemstones on the wire. String ½–1" of Hill Tribes silver cube beads on each end.

step 2

Crimp one end of the necklace to the loop on a hook clasp.

step 3

Crimp the other end of the necklace to an extender chain. Attach a 20mm CZ drop to the end of the extender chain with a wrapped loop (see step 6 for details on making a wrapped loop over this type of bead).

step 4

Cut the fine-link cable chain into three pieces: 1", ⅜", and ⅝". Open the connector loop on the enhancer bail and attach the end links of each chain segment.

step 5

String a 20mm drop on the 24-gauge wire and bend the wire ends over the drop as shown. The short end doesn't need to be more than about ½" long.

step 6

Bend both ends of the wire so they are parallel and vertical.

step 7

Make a loop using the long end of the wire. Trim the other wire end just below the loop.

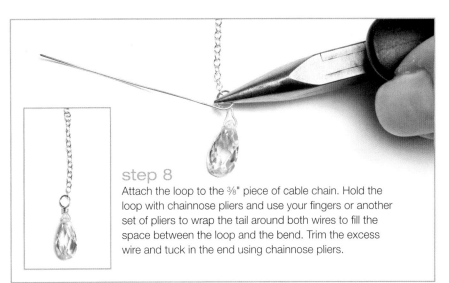

step 8
Attach the loop to the ⅜" piece of cable chain. Hold the loop with chainnose pliers and use your fingers or another set of pliers to wrap the tail around both wires to fill the space between the loop and the bend. Trim the excess wire and tuck in the end using chainnose pliers.

step 9
Attach another 20mm drop to the ⅝" chain in the same way.

step 10
To attach the largest drop, string it on the remaining 24-gauge wire, bend the wire ends over the drop as before, and bend both ends of the wire so that they are parallel and vertical. Wrap one of the wires around the other two or three times and trim the end. String the cone and a Hill Tribes silver cube over the remaining wire. Connect it to the 1" chain with a wrapped loop,

earrings
The earring drops are made in the same way you created the pendant drops in the previous step. Attach the earring drops to the connector loops on the earring wires.

Variation

The same dress inspired this bracelet.

Fantasy Pod
necklace

materials
- 30mm oval melon agate bead with eight grooves
- 7 8mm crystal cubes
- 22 4mm crystal rondelles
- 8 3mm crystal rounds
- 40 2mm crystal rounds
- 5 grams 11º charlottes
- 2 grams 13º charlottes
- 4mm daisy spacer
- Flexible beading wire
- 15 antique-brass square bead caps (to fit 8mm cubes)
- 16" 28-gauge gunmetal-color wire
- Two-tone ball headpin
- 5mm antique-brass jump ring
- 2 black base metal crimp beads
- Antique-brass toggle clasp

tools
- Chainnose pliers
- Flatnose pliers
- Roundnose pliers
- Wire cutters
- Crimping pliers

When I was five years old I saw my first poppy pod. The tiny poppy seeds rattling inside amazed me. Pods seem like perfectly designed little treasure boxes, each containing a new wonder. Some are as small as a grain of sand and some are large and smooth, like polished mahogany. They grow in a multitude of intricately detailed shapes. Sometimes they are divided into chambers; sometimes they are shaped like a flower bud. Sometimes they have thorns to protect the precious treasure inside.

The beauty of pods—their outer as well as hidden beauty—inspired this project. While it's not meant to literally replicate a specific kind of pod, the shape of the focal piece is reminiscent of the pod of the poppy flower. I chose an agate melon bead because its shape is similar to a pod, and the grooves lend themselves well to embellishment. The bead cap at the base of the piece enhances the podlike quality of the pendant and is a practical way to anchor the beaded wires.

Sparkling charlottes are sometimes referred to as "one-cuts" or "true-cuts." A standard 20" hank of 11º Czech glass charlottes weighs about 34 grams and holds about 4300 beads. A standard 6" hank of 13º charlottes weighs about 13 grams and holds about 3500 beads.

step 1
String the daisy spacer, the bead cap, and the agate melon bead on the headpin and make a wrapped loop.

step 2
Cut the gunmetal-colored wire into four 4" pieces. Bend one of the pieces in the center and wrap it securely around the wrap of the wrapped loop.

step 3
String charlottes and crystals onto the wire, beginning with 13º charlottes.

step 4
String charlottes and crystals to span the bead. I strung seven 13º charlottes in step 3 and then a pattern of 11º charlotte, 2mm crystal, 11º, and two 13º charlottes. Repeat the pattern until you reach the top of the bead, string a 3mm crystal, and pass the wire through the closest opening on the bead cap.

step 5
Wrap several tight loops around the side of the bead cap. Wrap the end of the wire below the loops and above the crystal to make a wrapped loop. Trim the wire.

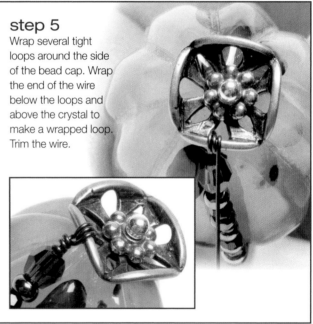

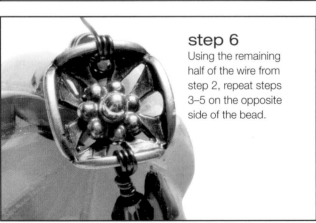

step 6
Using the remaining half of the wire from step 2, repeat steps 3–5 on the opposite side of the bead.

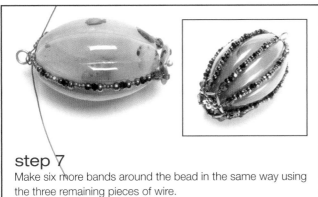

step 7

Make six more bands around the bead in the same way using the three remaining pieces of wire.

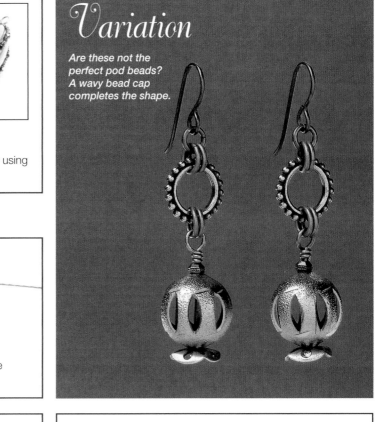

Variation

Are these not the perfect pod beads? A wavy bead cap completes the shape.

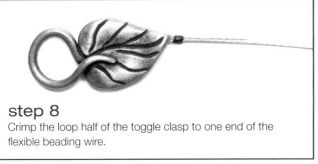

step 8

Crimp the loop half of the toggle clasp to one end of the flexible beading wire.

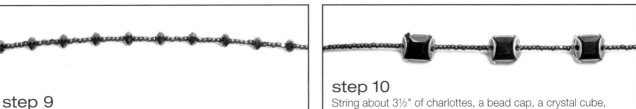

step 9

String five 11º charlottes (about ¼") and a faceted bead. Repeat the pattern until you have used all of the faceted beads.

step 10

String about 3½" of charlottes, a bead cap, a crystal cube, and another bead cap. String in this pattern: ⅜–½" of charlottes, bead cap, cube, and bead cap until you have strung all of the cubes.

step 11

String nine charlottes. Crimp the toggle bar to the end of the flexible beading wire.

step 12

Use a jump ring to attach the beaded pod pendant to the toggle loop.

Hawaiian Isles
bracelet

materials
- 30–40 assorted 5–14mm shell and semiprecious stone flower beads
- 10–12 6mm Swarovski margaritas
- 8–10 4mm crystal bicones
- 15–20 assorted side-drilled stones and CZs
- 3 5mm pearls
- 2 copper spacers
- 2 copper mesh chain end findings
- 3–5' 28-gauge copper wire
- 6–8" copper mesh chain
- 30–40 1½" copper ball headpins
- 4 copper jump rings
- Copper floral toggle clasp

tools
- Chainnose pliers
- Flatnose pliers
- Nylon-jaw pliers
- Roundnose pliers
- Wire cutters

TONY MIECH

As soon as I step off the airplane in the Hawaiian islands, the first thing I always notice is the scent. I'm overwhelmed by the beautiful smell of flowers. As I start to travel to my hotel, I see exotic, lush blooms everywhere. The sidewalks, the beaches, the hillsides— all are full of the most gorgeous colors and shapes of flowers.

One of the most intriguing things about Hawaii is the contrast in climate from region to region. Hawaii is often described as lush, and it does have many beautiful tropical areas, but it also has dry places and fields of dark lava. I love the contrast between the black sand beaches and the gorgeous verdant green of the landscape with swathes of colorful blossoms.

This piece reflects those contrasts. I chose a darker background to recall the lava fields, and I selected beads that reminded me of the shapes of Hawaiian flowers. I was fortunate to find quite a few beads that resembled plumeria, heliconia, and passionflower. Using pictures of Hawaiian flowers as inspiration, I selected pink and green tourmaline. The white and yellow flowers echo the plumeria blooms, and I included CZs in heliconia shapes and crystals in tropical colors. I added wire spirals that suggest the different vines that I saw. I finished the bracelet with a floral clasp that continues the theme.

step 1

Cut a piece of mesh chain about 1½" shorter than the desired bracelet size. Insert one end of the chain as far as it will go into an end finding.

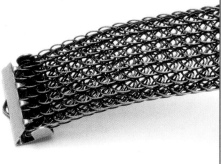

step 2

Using nylon-jaw pliers, squeeze the finding in the center.

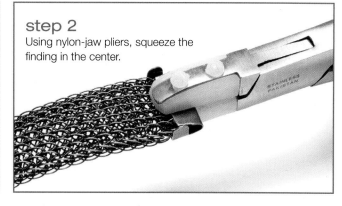

step 3

Fold over the side flaps and squeeze them with nylon-jaw pliers. Attach the other end finding in the same way.

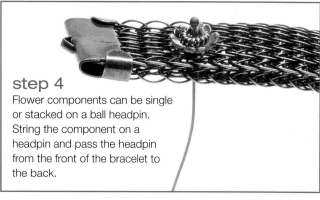

step 4

Flower components can be single or stacked on a ball headpin. String the component on a headpin and pass the headpin from the front of the bracelet to the back.

step 5

Bend the headpin upward and pass it through from back to front so the end exits very close to the component. Form a tight spiral with the end of the ball headpin.

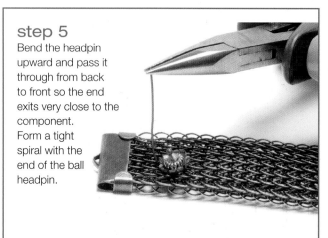

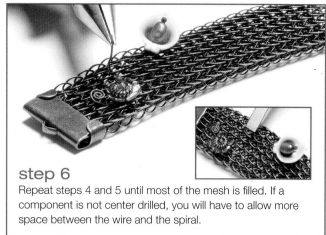

step 6

Repeat steps 4 and 5 until most of the mesh is filled. If a component is not center drilled, you will have to allow more space between the wire and the spiral.

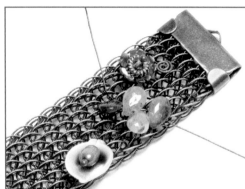

step 7

Fill in by adding crystals and side-drilled stones. To add the side-drilled stones, wrap a wire end several times around one of the links of mesh chain. String the crystals or stone beads, and then wrap the wire again around one of the links at the edge of the bracelet.

step 8

Use a jump ring to connect half of the clasp on each end.

Variation

Flattened bead caps provide a neat finish to the mesh in this necklace version.

Victorian Cameo
necklace

materials

- 45mm antique-brass filigree component with 8 petals
- 25x32mm oval vintage glass cameo
- 15 8x20mm matte onyx beads
- 6mm matte onyx round bead
- 1" fine-link antique-brass chain
- 22-gauge antique-brass headpin
- 15 22-gauge antique-brass eyepins
- 8mm antique-brass textured jump ring
- 19 4mm antique-brass jump rings
- Antique brass lobster-claw clasp
- 2" large-link, antique-brass chain for extender

tools

- Chainnose pliers
- Flatnose pliers
- Roundnose pliers
- Wire cutters
- Metal file

TONY MIECH

Queen Victoria was the first person to popularize mourning jewelry when she began wearing black clothing and jewelry after the death of her beloved husband, Prince Albert. She created a trend that lasted several decades.

Mourning jewelry often has an immediately recognizable look, even though the materials used to create it varied widely. One of the most popular materials was jet, but artists also used onyx, enamel on gold, horn, and even gutta percha, a dark-colored latex made from trees. Some mourning jewelry was not dark or black, and instead was made of other stones like banded sardonyx. Some of it incorporated pearls to contrast against the black.

I've always found the look of mourning jewelry striking. The Victorians' use of delicate cameos in ornate settings and the visually bold combination of dark colors with gold creates memorable jewelry.

For this design, I stayed close to the aesthetic of the necklace that was its inspiration because the clean lines appealed to me and seemed timeless, even though the piece is more than 100 years old. I chose hand-carved matte onyx beads and a vintage glass cameo that is slightly matte with a polished background. I also drew inspiration from other mourning jewelry, placing the cameo in an ornate setting, for example.

step 1

Use flatnose pliers to flatten the curved petals of the filigree setting.

step 2

Cut away unneeded sections of the filigree setting to create seven prongs. Leave the eighth petal intact.

step 3

Use a metal file to smooth any rough edges on the component.

step 4

Position the cameo on the back of the setting, placing the petal at the top. Use a fine-tip permanent marker to mark each prong around the edge of the cameo.

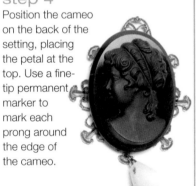

step 5

Grasp the prongs just outside the marked line with flatnose pliers and bend to a 90-degree angle.

step 6

Insert the cameo in the setting, check the fit, and make any necessary adjustments. Use flatnose pliers to tighten each prong by bending it over the edge of the cameo as far as it will go.

step 7

Working from the back, insert a 4mm jump ring through the top of the intact petal.

step 8

Bend the petal forward over the edge of the cameo.

step 9
Attach an eyepin to the jump ring on the cameo component. String a large onyx bead on the eyepin and make another loop above the bead.

step 10
Attach a 4mm jump ring to the top loop. Attach a textured jump ring to the 4mm jump ring using two 4mm jump rings. Use a 4mm jump ring to attach a ½" piece of chain to the textured jump ring.

step 11
On each end, attach an eyepin to the last link of the chain, string a large onyx bead, make a loop, and attach the loop to a 4mm jump ring.

step 12
On each end, continue to attach links made this way until you reach 8", not including the chain.

step 13
One one end, attach a lobster-claw clasp with a jump ring.

step 14
On the other end, attach an extender chain with a jump ring. String a 6mm round onyx bead on a headpin and attach it to the end of the extender chain with a wrapped loop.

Variation

Many Victorian mourning jewelry pieces featured a floral motif.

Splendor
bracelet & earrings

materials

- 3 18mm ceramic focal beads
- 5 4mm round crystals
- 2 grams 11º cylinder beads in background color
- 2 grams 11º cylinder beads in three accent colors
- 3 15º seed beads or charlottes
- 2 daisy charms
- 5 daisy spacers
- 11" 20-gauge gold-filled wire
- 18" 26-gauge gold-filled wire
- 7 8mm antique-copper jump rings
- 12 4–5mm antique-brass jump rings
- 3 antique-copper ball headpins
- Beading thread
- Antique-brass toggle clasp
- Pair of gold-filled earring wires

tools & supplies

- Chainnose pliers
- Flatnose pliers
- Roundnose pliers
- Wire cutters
- Beading needle
- Chasing hammer
- Steel bench block
- GS-Hypo Cement
- Scissors

Gustav Klimt's paintings are so moving and visually rich; his work conveys striking passion and energy. He uses different metallic colors such as golds, bronzes, and coppers, and his color palette and shapes are very easily translated into adornment. There's a natural relationship between his work and jewelry design.

I connect with Klimt's style not only because of his choice of color but also because of the organic elements that he favors. He often uses nature as his inspiration, reinterpreting it and painting it in a dreamy, stylized manner.

This piece was inspired by Klimt's style in general as well as particular paintings, such as "The Kiss" (above) and "Accomplishment." I was fortunate to find hand-painted beads that were obviously inspired by Klimt. For the bracelet, I made spirals from gold-filled wire to reflect the spirals in his paintings. I used a variety of cylinder beads in the colors that Klimt painted with to create miniature canvases in geometric shapes. I added a few small flowers, which echo flowers found in his paintings. I embellished with accents of different metallic colors and warm earth tones. Lastly, the clasp finishes the bracelet with another spiral element.

peyote components, step 1

On a threaded needle, pick up 12 cylinders, leaving a 12" tail. These beads will become rows one and two as you stitch row three.

step 2

To begin row three, pick up a bead and sew back through the second-last bead from the previous step. (To "sew back through" means going through a bead added earlier, this time moving in the opposite direction.) Continue to stitch row three by picking up a bead, skipping a bead in the previous row, and sewing back through the next bead.

When you finish row three, pull the thread taut. The beads should appear to be stacked like bricks with six raised beads.

To stitch row four, pick up a bead and sew through the first raised bead of the previous row, filling in the gap.

tip Design the color-blocked peyote components as you stitch. Use mostly background-color cylinders with small individual beads or blocks of beads in accent colors interspersed.

step 3

This photo shows nine rows complete (count beads on the diagonal). Continue in peyote stitch until you have completed 13 rows.

step 4

Sew through the peyote component and exit where you would like to place a daisy spacer. It's a good idea to place the daisy spacer so that it is one to two rows away from the path of the wire (see steps 2 and 3 of assembling the bracelet). Pick up a spacer and a 15º seed bead or charlotte, and sew back through the daisy spacer. Sew through the cylinder the thread is exiting to anchor the daisy spacer above it. Reinforce the thead path a few times to secure the spacer to the cylinder.

Sew both thread tails back into the peyote component, following the original thread path and tying half-hitch knots as you go. If desired, place a dot of glue on the final knots and trim the ends.

Make two additional peyote components.

spirals, step 1

Cut a 2½" piece of 20-gauge wire. Make a loose spiral with an open center. Use a chasing hammer on a steel bench block to hammer the spiral so it is slightly flattened.

step 2

Make a loop at the end of the spiral and hammer it as well.

step 3

Because the loop may open up slightly as you flatten it, use flatnose pliers to make any necessary adjustments so the spiral is even.

Make another spiral component.

bracelet assembly, step 1

Cut the 26-gauge wire into 3" pieces. Pass one piece through the fourth or fifth row from the top of a peyote component.

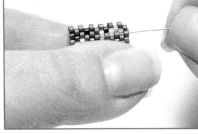

step 2

Make a wrapped loop on each side.

step 3

String another wire through row 9 or 10 of the same peyote component and make a wrapped loop on each side.

Repeat steps 1–3 for the two remaining peyote components.

step 4

String the focal bead onto the remaining 20-gauge wire. Make a plain loop on each side.

step 5

For both spiral components, attach a pair of small antique brass jump rings to the spiral and to the loop at the end of the spiral.

step 6

Connect a pair of small antique brass jump rings to both halves of the clasp. Use 8mm copper jump rings to connect all of the components, including the clasp halves. See p. 72 for the order of all the components.

step 7

String a 4mm crystal round onto a headpin. Make a wrapped loop to attach it to the large jump ring next to the toggle ring. Repeat to make three dangles.

earrings

Make a plain loop and attach a daisy charm. String a 4mm crystal, a daisy spacer, and a focal bead onto the wire. Make a second loop, attaching it to the earring wire. Make a second earring.

Variation

A copper spiral component helps to carry out the theme in this necklace.

CallaLily
necklace

materials

- 38mm copper disk
- 38mm Hill Tribes silver stamen component
- 9mm Hill Tribes silver leaf charm
- 6mm antique copper cube beads
- 4mm antique copper cube beads
- 20–24 2mm antique copper round beads
- 18–20 Hill Tribes silver barbell beads
- 280–300 2mm Hill Tribes silver beads
- 3 8mm Hill Tribes silver textured rings
- Flexible beading wire
- 24-gauge antique-copper headpin
- 2 5mm sterling silver jump rings
- 2 sterling silver crimp beads
- Antique-copper hook clasp
- 2" antique-copper chain for extender

tools & supplies

- Chainnose pliers
- Flatnose pliers
- Roundnose pliers
- Nylon jaw pliers
- Wire cutters
- Crimping pliers
- Liver of sulfur

I was always aware of calla lilies, even at a very young age. My mother would point them out as they were blooming, and I loved the elegant white flowers and how they seemed just a little mysterious. When we moved from Russia to the United States, I was amazed to discover other gorgeous colors of calla lilies—yellow, orange, pink, and mauve.

The grace and elegance of the calla lily makes it the perfect flower for formal occasions. Georgia O'Keeffe, Diego Rivera, and others captured its beauty in many of their famous paintings.

In this design, I have emulated the flow and curve of a calla lily in copper, and added bright silver and antique copper accents. A Hill Tribes silver component acts as the stamen, and a small leaf rests at the base of the flower.

step 1

Shape the copper disk with your fingers, beginning to fold it in half but not completely flattening it. Use flatnose pliers to sharply crease the fold on one end.

step 2

Place the copper shape on a steel bench block and strike the end with a chasing hammer to flatten and sharpen the crease. This crease will be at the base of the pendant, which represents the wide opening of the lily.

step 3

Use nylon-jaw pliers to open the shape and create curves as shown, working from the crease upward and folding one side over the other. Leave the opening at the top of the copper component large enough so the loop at the end of the stamen component can pass through it.

Add patina to the copper using a liver of sulfur solution.

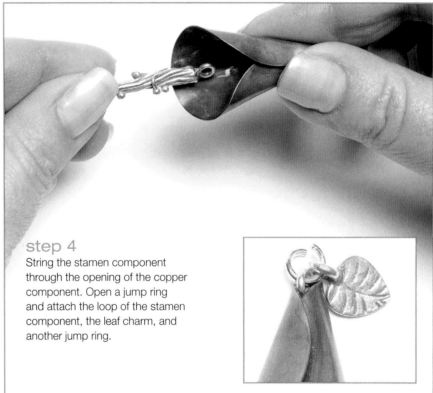

step 4

String the stamen component through the opening of the copper component. Open a jump ring and attach the loop of the stamen component, the leaf charm, and another jump ring.

step 5

Cut a 20" piece of flexible beading wire and string the calla lily pendant to the center of the wire. On one side of the pendant, string 9" of beads, alternating 2mm Hill Tribes silver beads, 2mm antique copper rounds, silver barbells, and 4mm and 6mm copper cubes.

step 6

On the other end of the beading wire, string 9" of beads, alternating 2mm Hill Tribes silver beads with sections of 4mm and 6mm copper cubes. Between several of these sections, string a Hill Tribes silver ring as shown.

step 7

Crimp the jump ring of the hook clasp to one end of the beading wire.

step 8

Crimp the extender chain to the other end of the beading wire. On a headpin, string a 2mm copper round, a 5mm copper cube, and a 2mm copper round. Attach to the last link of the extender chain with a wrapped loop.

Variation

This calla lily is made of metal clay.

Globetrotter
necklace

materials

- Stamp pendant
- Vintage or reproduction coin with center opening
- 12mm fine silver bead
- Fine silver charm
- Assorted semiprecious stone beads, 4–15mm
- 5½" 22-gauge half-hard sterling silver wire
- 14" large-link sterling silver chain
- 2 7mm sterling silver jump rings
- 12 6mm copper jump rings
- 2 sterling silver double-wall crimp tubes
- Sterling silver hook clasp

tools

- Chainnose pliers
- Roundnose pliers
- Wire cutters
- Screw-action metal punch (for ³⁄₃₂" and ¹⁄₁₆" holes)
- Center punch
- Bench block
- Riveting hammer

TONY MIECH

Travel can be magical—a renewing well of inspiration. When you leave your familiar, everyday environment to venture to a new place, you're immersed in a different world and surrounded by fresh visual imagery. You're more attentive to the sights around you because you have entered an unfamiliar landscape.

When I'm traveling, I love to drink in the atmosphere. I want to remember every moment and savor every blade of grass and every leaf on every tree. I want to see the native wildlife and explore the rivers and forests. I want to see the sunset and find the most beautiful flowers in the area.

Traveling to Australia with my family was a wonderful experience. The most memorable part of my journey was interacting with kangaroos and other marsupials in a specially designed habitat. They're quite gentle and have such personality.

For this necklace, the iconic kangaroo pendant seemed like the perfect image to recall my travels there. Made from a postage stamp, the pendant also shows how beautifully stark much of the landscape is. The elements in the necklace represent the colors of the landscape. I included opal in the mix because it's native to Australia.

step 1

With the fine-tip marker, mark two points on the coin opposite each other, approximately 2mm from the edge.

step 2

Use the ³⁄₃₂" screw (usually black) to pierce holes at the marks. Look through the hole in the bottom of the punch to align the screw with the mark.

step 3

Place a crimp tube upright on the bench block. Position the center punch on top of the crimp tube and gently tap the punch with a riveting hammer until one end of the tube is slightly flared.

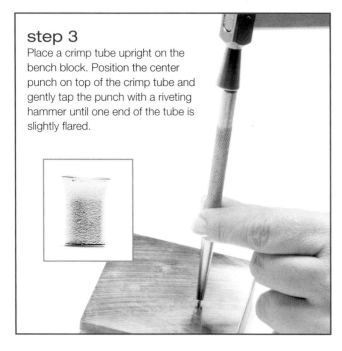

step 4

Turn the crimp over. Place the coin on top of it so the tube is in one of the holes, flared end down.

step 5

Use the punch and the riveting hammer to slightly flare the other end of the tube. Use the riveting hammer to tap gently on both ends of the tube until it flattens into a rivet around the hole. Make a second tube rivet in the other hole.

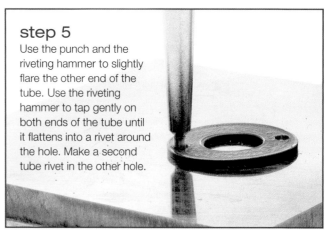

step 6

Cut the large-link chain into four pieces: 1", 1½", 3", and 8". Attach the pendant to the shortest pieces of chain with a jump ring.

step 7

Use a jump ring to attach the end link of the 1" piece of chain to the riveted coin. Attach a jump ring and the 8" piece of chain to the other tube-riveted hole.

step 8

Use two copper jump rings to attach a charm to the end link of chain.

step 9

On the other end, create wrapped-loop bead components and alternate them with doubled copper jump rings. Attach the 3" piece of chain to the last pair of jump rings.

step 10

Attach two copper jump rings to the last link of chain. Attach the hook to the copper rings with a large silver jump ring.

Variation

The gardens and fairy-tale cottages of Cape Cod inspired this necklace.

Twisting Vine
bracelet

materials

- 5 5mm shell flowers
- 7 3mm round CZ beads
- 7 3mm antique bronze melon beads
- 3 3mm freshwater pearls
- 36" 18-gauge sterling silver or silver-plated wire
- 1–3' 24-gauge sterling silver or silver-plated wire
- 1–3' 22-gauge sterling silver or silver-plated wire
- 1–3' 20-gauge copper wire
- 1–3' 24-gauge antique-brass wire
- 5 1½" copper ball headpins

tools

- Chainnose pliers
- Stepped forming pliers with 5mm, 7mm, and 10mm steps
- Wire cutters
- Bracelet pliers
- Chasing hammer
- Bench block
- Liver of sulfur (optional)

The natural world has long been one of my keen interests. Trees, plants, leaves…I love studying them, identifying them, and appreciating them.

Gnarled plant life fascinates me, particularly when I glimpse it in lovely old gardens. Over the years, trees and vines twist and turn, intertwining and growing ever more interesting as they embrace each other. As the light touches them, the scene can turn magical, especially if flowers are blooming on the vines.

On the way to work in my bead store every day, I pass through a nature conservancy. It's lush and overgrown, and a brook flows through the middle of it. One summer I noticed what looked like flowers blooming on the trunks of some of the trees. As I looked more closely, I realized that a wild vine had grown around the tree. Its white flowers caught the light like brilliant stars dotting the dark bark.

I was inspired to create a bracelet that would mimic the natural bends of the wild vine and the look of tree bark. I varied the thickness of the wire and darkened it with liver of sulfur to give the bracelet an organic look. Shell flowers add a floral note and sparkling green CZs suggest the forest at dusk. Pearls contribute depth and color, and antique bronze melon beads create additional texture.

Variation

Enameled flower components are the focal point of this fibula.

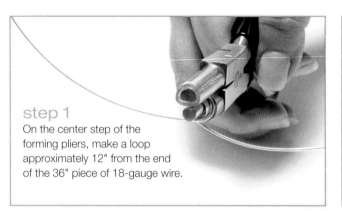

step 1

On the center step of the forming pliers, make a loop approximately 12" from the end of the 36" piece of 18-gauge wire.

step 2

Hold the loop with flatnose pliers and wrap one end of the wire loosely around the other several times at the base of the loop.

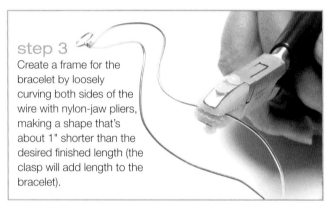

step 3

Create a frame for the bracelet by loosely curving both sides of the wire with nylon-jaw pliers, making a shape that's about 1" shorter than the desired finished length (the clasp will add length to the bracelet).

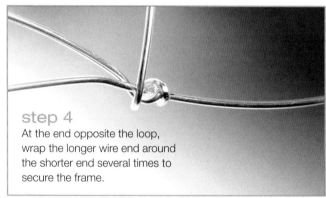

step 4

At the end opposite the loop, wrap the longer wire end around the shorter end several times to secure the frame.

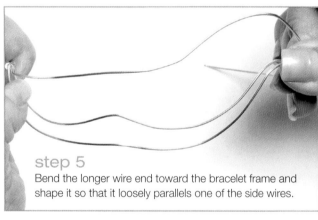

step 5

Bend the longer wire end toward the bracelet frame and shape it so that it loosely parallels one of the side wires.

step 6

Wrap the wire around the loop side of the frame to secure it.

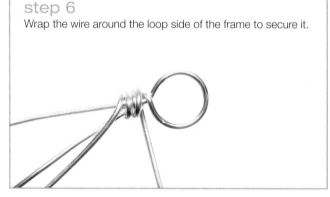

step 7

Add wires of different colors and gauges by wrapping a new piece between the coils already in the frame.

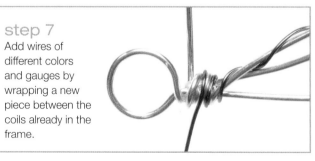

step 8

Secure the end of the new wire by tucking it between the coiled wire with chainnose pliers.

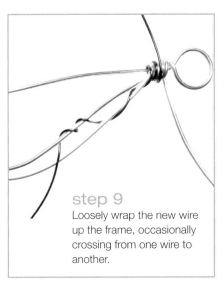

step 9
Loosely wrap the new wire up the frame, occasionally crossing from one wire to another.

step 10
Embellish by adding beads occasionally to the 24- and 22-gauge wires as you wrap. Continue to layer wires to build up the "vines," sometimes crossing from one side to the other to add interest and reinforce the bracelet at the same time.

step 11
To add flower beads, string a flower bead on a headpin and tightly wrap the headpin around a vine. Tuck the ends of the headpins between the wires.

step 12
Add and wrap more wires and beaded headpins as desired to reinforce the bracelet. Secure all the wire ends by wrapping them around other wires and tucking the ends between wires.

step 13
On the other end of the bracelet, bend the unfinished wire end into a hook on the largest step of the forming pliers.

step 14
Use chainnose pliers to bend the end of the hook as shown. Trim the wire end to leave just a tiny U shape.

step 15
Use the tip of the chainnose pliers to press the wire end tightly against the hook.

step 16
Place the hook on the steel bench block and strike with a chasing hammer to flatten and strengthen the wire. Do the same with the loop.

step 17
Twist the loop so it's perpendicular to the hook. Use nylon-jaw bracelet pliers to shape the bracelet into a circle. Add patina using liver of sulfur if desired.

Botanical Tiles
bracelet

CHERYL WATT

When I first saw Cheryl Watt's artwork, it was clear that we share a very big source of inspiration: the natural world. So many of her designs could inspire jewelry!

Cheryl's Breezy Boxed Botanicals immediately draws the viewer in, depicting an imaginative and richly colored garden as seen through a window. She carves each piece of the work in clay and colors them with metallic acrylic paints.

For this piece, I chose copper as the background to reflect the warm tones of Cheryl's artwork. Each tile in the bracelet is textured differently, and the botanical elements are offset, just as they are in the artwork. It was fun to find and, in some cases, alter botanical components that would complete this design. For example, I had to hammer bead caps into a flat shape, cut off unnecessary loops, and use only part of a component—all part of the enjoyable challenge of designing this bracelet.

materials

- 6 20mm square copper blanks
- 6–12 assorted antique-brass components
- 6–8 2mm crystal rounds
- 6 daisy spacers
- 18–24" 26-gauge gold-filled wire
- 24 8mm antique copper jump rings
- 8 6mm antique brass jump rings
- Antique-copper toggle clasp

tools

- Chainnose pliers
- Flatnose pliers
- Wire cutters
- Texturing hammer
- Dead-blow hammer
- Steel bench block
- Metal stamps
- Hole-punching pliers
- Liver of sulfur

step 1

Use a texturing hammer to texture three of the copper blanks on the bench block.

step 2

Use various metal stamps to texture the remaining copper blanks. Place a blank on the bench block and strike each stamp firmly with a dead-blow hammer.

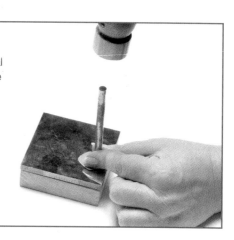

step 3

Use a fine-tip permanent marker to mark placement for four connector holes on each blank as shown.

step 4

Use hole-punching pliers to make holes in each copper blank. Use liver of sulfur to add patina to the copper blanks.

step 5

Determine the position of each antique brass component on each copper blank and decide how and where you plan to attach it. Components will be secured to holes in the blanks with wire.

step 6

Mark the positions where you intend to punch holes to connect the elements and use the punching pliers to make the holes.

attaching flower components, step 1

Cut a 5" piece of wire and string a 2mm crystal. Bend the wire around the bead and make a 90-degree angle bend where the two wire ends meet.

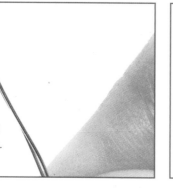

step 2

String both ends of the wire through a daisy spacer, a flower component, and the hole in the copper blank, and spread the ends to point in opposite directions.

step 3
Secure the wire ends by wrapping each end several times through a hole on opposite sides of the copper blank.

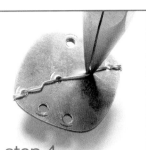

step 4
On the back of the component, use chainnose pliers to add a few small Z-bends in the wire: Grasp the wire with the tip and rotate the pliers slightly. This will take up slack in the wire to make a tighter attachment.

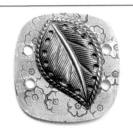

step 5
Adapt the technique to each component as you continue. For example, to attach the leaf component, pass the wire through at least two openings on opposite sides of the component. Secure the ends by wrapping through the holes at the edge of the copper blank.

bracelet assembly, step 1
Attach an 8mm copper jump ring to each of the four connector holes of each bracelet component.

step 2
Connect all of the components with 6mm brass jump rings.

step 3
Attach the toggle bar with a chain of two brass jump rings.

Variation
The tile-like component echoes the pendant's theme within the chain.

step 4
Attach the toggle loop with a brass jump ring.

Gerbera Daisy
pendant

materials
- 40mm round copper blank
- 15-loop brass filigree component
- About 50 3mm crystal bicones in assorted colors
- 2 grams 13° charlottes
- 18" 26-gauge gold-filled wire
- Fireline beading thread
- Brass mesh

tools
- Chainnose pliers
- Wire cutters
- Hole-punching pliers
- Nylon-jaw pliers
- Texturing hammer with line pattern
- Steel bench block
- Metal shears
- Liver of sulfur
- Beading needle

I love the cheerful exuberance of gerbera daisies and their warm, vivid colors. These beautiful daisies have always been my mother's favorite flower, and I have fond memories of the summer she grew them on her balcony. They brighten any room.

Gerbera daisies come in warm hues such as pink and orange, so I decided to use copper as the base of this piece. I chose crystals in colors that reminded me of the daisies. I purposely made the flower petals very irregular, because on a real flower no two petals are exactly alike. So don't try for perfection in your flower—embrace the beautiful imperfections that make it organic, just like the real thing.

DREAMSTIME

step 1

Use a fine-tip permanent marker to draw 15 lines around the perimeter of the copper disk, dividing it into petals. Each line should be 8–9mm long.

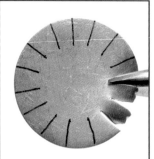

step 2

Use metal shears to snip out space between the petals and to make a small divot in the center of each petal as shown.

step 3

Place the piece on a steel bench block. Strike it with the texturing hammer to texture the petals.

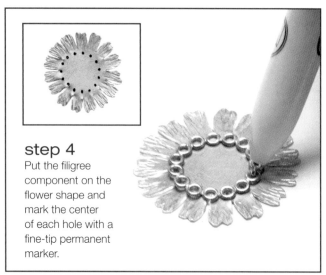

step 4

Put the filigree component on the flower shape and mark the center of each hole with a fine-tip permanent marker.

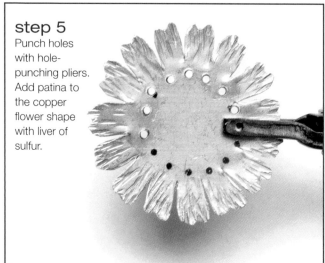

step 5

Punch holes with hole-punching pliers. Add patina to the copper flower shape with liver of sulfur.

step 6
Use nylon-jaw pliers to curve the tips of the petals.

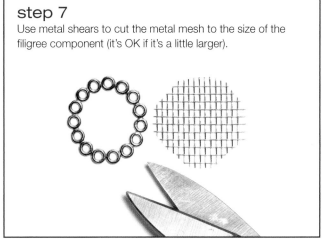

step 7
Use metal shears to cut the metal mesh to the size of the filigree component (it's OK if it's a little larger).

step 8
Use chainnose pliers to remove some of the outer wires on the mesh component, exposing longer end wires.

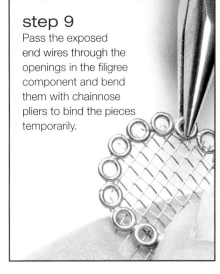

step 9
Pass the exposed end wires through the openings in the filigree component and bend them with chainnose pliers to bind the pieces temporarily.

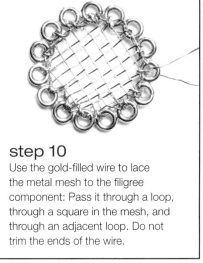

step 10
Use the gold-filled wire to lace the metal mesh to the filigree component: Pass it through a loop, through a square in the mesh, and through an adjacent loop. Do not trim the ends of the wire.

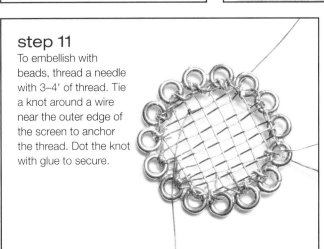

step 11
To embellish with beads, thread a needle with 3–4' of thread. Tie a knot around a wire near the outer edge of the screen to anchor the thread. Dot the knot with glue to secure.

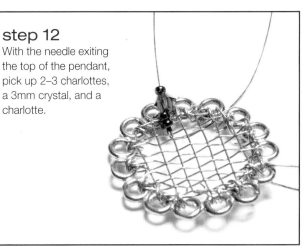

step 12
With the needle exiting the top of the pendant, pick up 2–3 charlottes, a 3mm crystal, and a charlotte.

step 13

Skip the last charlotte added and sew back through the crystal, the charlottes, and the screen.

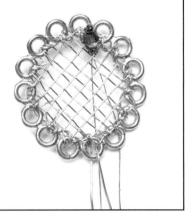

step 14

Sew up through the adjacent square on the screen and repeat step 12 and 13. Complete the outer round in this way and then fill in the center. Tie a knot close to the screen, dot with glue, and bring the thread through one of the beaded strands to exit the top. Trim the excess thread.

step 15

String the ends of the gold-filled wire through two holes in the copper flower.

step 16

Use both ends of the wire to string through an adjacent hole in the flower and the beaded component.

step 17

Keep passing the wire front to back and back to front to sew the beaded component to the flower.

step 18

After you have completed the full circle, continue sewing through the two components to reinforce the piece. Wrap the end of the wire neatly around another part of the wire on the back of the piece. Trim the excess wire and tuck the end toward the back of the pendant.

step 19

Make a hole in one of the petals using a hole-punching pliers. Connect the pendant to the bail with a jump ring.

Variation

A crystal component adds sparkle to a gerbera daisy pendant.

Nouveau Elegance

necklace & earrings

materials

- 12x28mm antique-brass rectangular focal component
- 3 16mm 8-petal antique-brass flower components
- 3 8mm square CZs
- 2 freshwater pearls
- 6 3.5mm round peridot beads
- 18" antique-brass fine-link cable chain
- 2 antique-brass headpins
- 6 antique-brass eyepins
- 12 4mm antique-brass jump rings
- Antique-brass hook clasp
- 2" large-link antique brass chain with unsoldered links for extender
- Pair of antique-brass earring wires

tools

- Chainnose pliers
- Flatnose pliers
- Roundnose pliers
- Wire cutters
- Nylon-jaw bracelet-forming pliers

The Art Nouveau period, known for a stylized organic look that was often based on natural inspiration, began at the turn of the 20th century. Art Nouveau jewelry embodies the look on a small scale with curved, flowing lines and specific color palettes.

Many of the jewelry designs of the day incorporated enamels and richly colored gemstones. Greens, lavenders, carmines, bright pastels, creams, and golds might all combine to create a lush, romantic look. Pearls were a favorite element, and many pieces feature baroque pearls in particular for their unusual shapes and texture.

I chose the inspiration piece for its classic Art Nouveau style and because I liked the combination of amethyst, peridot, and pearl. In my necklace, I turned a square stone on its side like a diamond to recall a common motif of the time. The lavender CZ fits the period's color theme. In order to create the setting for the CZ, I chose a reproduction vintage brass component that would reflect the style of the inspiration piece and introduce a floral element. I used a baroque pearl drop.

I liked the symmetry of my inspiration, which is why I picked a focal component to mirror the horizontal orientation of the focal component of the inspiration piece. This rectangular component is very reminiscent of Art Nouveau designs, although I made it a bit more three-dimensional to fit the period look.

necklace, step 1

Use chainnose pliers to bend the petals of the flower component upward and give it a slightly concave shape.

step 2

Use chainnose pliers to slightly bend the tip of every other petal into a prong that will hold the square CZ.

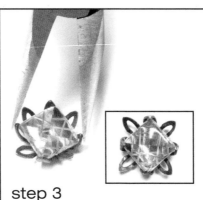

step 3

Place the CZ on the flower component with each corner aligning with a prong. Use chainnose pliers to grasp the setting at opposite corners of the stone. Squeeze tightly to bend the prongs over the corners. Move the pliers to the remaining pair of corners and squeeze to tighten them in the same way.

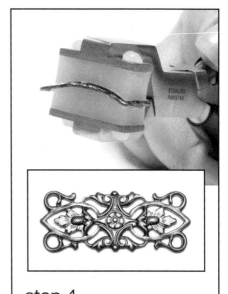

step 4

Use bracelet-forming pliers to curve the focal component.

step 5

Attach an eyepin to a corner hole of the focal component. String a peridot bead and make a loop on the other side of the bead. Connect three peridot bead components on each side of the focal component in this way.

step 6

Connect the last loop of each bottom peridot bead component to a petal on the stone setting as shown.

step 7

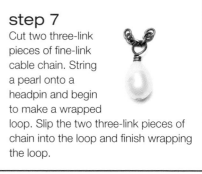

Cut two three-link pieces of fine-link cable chain. String a pearl onto a headpin and begin to make a wrapped loop. Slip the two three-link pieces of chain into the loop and finish wrapping the loop.

step 8

Use jump rings to connect the pearl-and-chain component to the focal component as shown.

step 9

Cut two 8" pieces of fine-link cable chain. On both sides of the focal component, use a jump ring to connect the chain to a hole in the component as shown.

step 10

On one end, connect a hook clasp to the last link of chain by opening the connector loop on the hook.

step 11

On the other end, open the end link of the large-link extender chain, connect it to the fine-link chain, and close the link. String a pearl on a headpin and attach it to the last line of the extender chain with a wrapped loop.

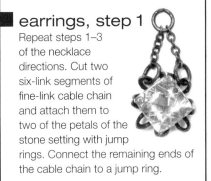

■ earrings, step 1

Repeat steps 1–3 of the necklace directions. Cut two six-link segments of fine-link cable chain and attach them to two of the petals of the stone setting with jump rings. Connect the remaining ends of the cable chain to a jump ring.

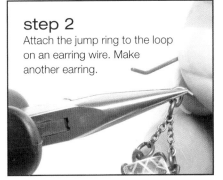

step 2

Attach the jump ring to the loop on an earring wire. Make another earring.

Variation

It's easy to create an Art Nouveau feeling with the many styles of vintage-look, antique-brass filigree components available today.

Timeless Gears
bracelet

materials

- 20–22mm diameter antique watch face
- 15x20mm antique-brass filigree bird
- 25mm diameter brass sprocket
- 22mm diameter silver sprocket with large center opening
- 21mm diameter silver sprocket
- 21mm diameter copper sprocket
- 19mm diameter silver sprocket with small center opening
- 19mm diameter brass sprocket
- 19mm diameter brass sprocket
- 12–14mm diameter vintage sprocket with post
- 14mm Swarovski crystal ring
- 3mm crystal round
- Half-drilled pearl
- 3' 28-gauge gunmetal wire
- 8" 26-gauge gold-filled wire
- 12–14 antique-brass and copper jump rings, assorted sizes and textures
- 6 10mm antique-brass jump rings
- Filigree toggle clasp

tools & supplies
- Chainnose pliers
- Flatnose pliers
- Wire cutters
- Two-part epoxy

Steampunk is a fascinating blend of futuristic fantasy with elements of Victorian design. Imagine a world where technology flourishes during the Industrial Revolution, where dirigibles and steam engines can coexist with computers. That is the world of steampunk—the future blended with the past.

In steampunk jewelry, utilitarian mechanisms such as gears and watch parts are combined with other unusual objects to create a futuristic yet antiquated look.

This bracelet was inspired not only by the steampunk style, but also by a reproduction clock that my husband and I purchased while on a trip. There's something romantic and old-fashioned about this device, as though it came out of the Victorian era.

I created the bracelet by combining old and new components. It includes an antique watch face. A sprocket with a sharp point became a great part of the design—the perfect place to attach a half-drilled pearl. I also used a bird component that reminded me of an antique clock decoration.

The rest of the parts are commercially made pieces that replicate gears or sprockets. I used a black crystal ring to reflect the background of the clock and to provide contrast among the antiqued copper and brass findings.

tip You'll find fun steampunk components like these at many bead stores. Look for gears, sprockets, and vintage and reproduction watch parts.

Variation

I love the unusual mix of elegant pearls and crystals with earthy, textural metals.

component 1, step 1

Cut two 5" pieces of 28-gauge gunmetal wire. Place the crystal ring on the 19mm brass sprocket. Starting in the center of one of the wire pieces, wrap the wire around both components three times, placing the wire wraps between the teeth of the sprocket.

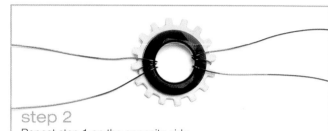

step 2

Repeat step 1 on the opposite side.

front

back

step 3

Place the wrapped crystal and gear on the copper sprocket. Use the remaining wire ends to securely wrap the three components together.

component 2, step 1

Cut a 15" piece of 28-gauge gunmetal wire. Place the silver sprocket with the small center opening on the 25mm brass sprocket. Pass the wire through the center of both pieces and wrap the wire between the teeth of the gear and through the openings in the sprocket. Move to the next opening and wrap again.

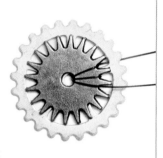

step 2

Continue working until you've wrapped around the entire gear.

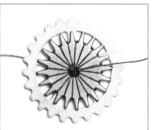

step 3

Bring one of the wires up through the center toward the top of the component, string a 3mm crystal round, and pass the wire back through the center opening toward the back of the piece.

step 4

Wrap both ends around any of the wires in the back.

component 3, step 1

Place the 12–14mm vintage sprocket on the 22mm silver sprocket with the large center opening. Use the 26-gauge gold-filled wire to wrap through the center of the sprocket and around the teeth. Go between all of the teeth and once around the sprocket until you have wrapped between all the teeth.

step 2

Wrap both wire ends tightly around any of the wires in the back.

step 3

Use two-part epoxy to adhere the pearl to the post on the sprocket. If there is a post on the back of the sprocket, use two-part epoxy to adhere a daisy spacer to the post.

component 4, step 1

Cut two 5" pieces of 28-gauge gunmetal wire. Place the filigree bird on the 19mm brass sprocket. Starting in the center of the wire, wrap around the edge of the filigree bird and through the teeth of the gear. Wrap this way at four points to secure.

step 2

Place the bird and sprocket on the 21mm silver sprocket. Use the remaining wire ends to securely wrap the bird and sprocket to the silver sprocket.

step 3

Wraps the wire ends around another wire on the back of the piece and tuck them toward the front.

bracelet assembly, step 1

Connect pairs of large antique-brass jump rings to each component on opposite sides whenever possible. Use single rings if necessary; the vintage watch face could accommodate only one jump ring on one side, for example.

step 2

Using 10mm antique-brass jump rings, connect components as shown. Use jump rings to attach the toggle clasp and loop as well.

Tree of Life
necklace

materials
- 32mm copper disk
- 15 4mm crystal bicones
- 3 leaf charms from leaf chain
- 17" antique-copper leaf chain
- 5 6mm antique-copper jump rings
- 15 antique-copper headpins
- 2 sterling silver double-wall crimp tubes
- Antique-copper hook clasp
- 2" antique-copper chain for extender

tools & supplies
- Chainnose pliers
- Flatnose pliers
- Roundnose pliers
- Wire cutters
- Screw-action metal punch
- Dead-blow hammer
- Chasing hammer (optional)
- Wooden dapping block (optional)
- Center punch
- Metal stamps, letter I and leaf
- Liver of sulfur

The tree of life is a beautiful and powerful image. Its legend says that all living beings dwell within this tree. Tree of life symbolism can be found in many different cultures, from the Yggdrasil in Norse mythology to the story of the Garden of Eden in the Bible.

The shape of the menorah, a sacred object in the Jewish tradition, is based on the tree of life. Contemporary artists who create menorahs continue to use the image of a tree because it resonates so deeply. The symbol of a tree is also connected to families. We speak of the roots of our history and the branches of our family tree.

Trees are all around us. I'm drawn to their beauty and how they provide shelter and even nourishment. Although trees are different in leaf and look, all have an innate strength and grace. The tree of life is such an elegant metaphor for the human experience and how we all are wrapped in its branches together.

There are many commercially available components that are designed as versions of the tree of life, but I decided it would be more meaningful to make my own. I used copper because of its warm color and how well it lends itself to a patina; I definitely wanted to antique the tree to add contrast. Copper leaf chain continues the tree motif. I wanted to give the necklace a bit of color and sparkle, so I chose a muted, natural color of crystal—smoky quartz—that blends well with the antiqued copper.

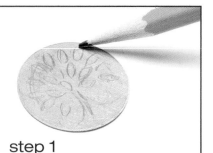

step 1

Use a pencil to draw the general shape of the tree on the copper disk. Then draw individual leaf shapes that are consistent with the size of the metal leaf stamp to guide you as you stamp.

step 2

Place the disk on the steel bench block, position the leaf stamp, and firmly strike the stamp once with a dead-blow hammer to stamp each leaf. Occasionally pause and redraw the pencil lines if they get erased.

step 3

Use the letter I stamp to create the tree trunk, roots, and branches, connecting each leaf to the tree in an organic way. These marks should appear very much like pencil strokes—they don't have to be precise.

step 4

Use the large ($\frac{3}{32}$") screw of the punch to make a hole at the top of the tree component.

step 5

Make another hole at the bottom of the component.

step 6

Make a tube rivet in the hole using a crimp tube: Place the tube upright on the bench block and position the center punch on top of the tube.

step 7

Gently tap the punch with a riveting hammer until one end of the tube is slightly flared.

step 8

Turn the crimp over. Place the tree component on top of it so the tube is in one of the holes, flared end down.

step 9

Use the punch and the riveting hammer to slightly flare the other end of the tube.

step 10

Use the riveting hammer to tap gently on both ends of the tube until it flattens into a rivet around the hole.

step 11

Make a second tube rivet in the other hole.

step 12

If you'd like to give your component a slightly domed shape, place it face down in a depression of the wooden dapping block that's slightly larger than the component and strike it gently a chasing hammer. Add patina to the tree component using liver of sulfur.

step 13

Use a jump ring to connect the tree component to the center of the chain. Use a jump ring to connect a single leaf to the riveted hole at the base of the tree component.

step 14

String a crystal onto a headpin and attach to the chain with a wrapped loop. Make 14 and space them ½" apart along the chain. Attach a crystal component to the bottom of the pendant.

step 15

One one end, attach the hook to the last chain link with a jump ring.

step 16

On the other end, attach the extender chain to the last chain link with a jump ring.

step 17

String a crystal on a headpin and make a wrapped-loop dangle. Attach two leaf charms and the dangle to the end of the extender chain with a jump ring.

Variation

I based this metal clay pendant on a sketch I made.

Acknowledgments

This book could not have been created without the assistance, time, and generosity of many wonderful people. I would like to thank my husband, Tony Miech, for being my steadfast travel companion for so many years, and for taking such stunning and inspirational pictures on our trips. I would like to thank my mother and father for instilling within me a love of nature and an appreciation of the natural world. Thank you to my boys, who so enthusiastically bring me an endless supply of pods and leaves and who are always full of the spirit of adventure in our travels. Thank you to Lauren Walsh for the use of the lovely wedding picture of her grandmother, and for her writing assistance.

My thanks also go out to:
Patty and Dorothy Gallun, who not only allowed me to photograph pieces from their amazing vintage jewelry collection, but also shared the history of the pieces and gave me a deeper understanding of the subject.
Tammy Rae Wolter for creating such inspiring, beautiful beads.
Pam Rehberg, who so generously spent her time researching Elizabethan portraits for me.
Mila Zinkova, who is not only a fantastic photographer, but who also shares my love of snorkeling and my birthplace.
Cheryl Watt, whose whimsical, colorful artwork was a wonderful inspiration. I thank her for allowing me to include it.
Tony Shafton, who shares my love of beach stones.
Sherill Schoening for allowing me to use one of her silk paintings, which captures the beauty of the water lily so perfectly.
Mary Plageman for generously providing me with a piece of Civil War mourning jewelry from her personal collection.

I would like to thank my editor, Mary Wohlgemuth, and the rest of the Kalmbach staff for their invaluable assistance. Thanks also to my wonderful store staff members for all of their enthusiastic help and continual support.

About the author

Irina Miech is an artist, teacher, and author. She also oversees her two retail stores, Eclectica and The Bead Studio, in Brookfield, Wisconsin, where she teaches classes in beading, wirework, and metal clay. Her jewelry designs have been featured in *Bead&Button*, *BeadStyle*, and *Art Jewelry* magazines. This is her seventh book.

Other books by Irina Miech
- *Metal Clay for Beaders*
- *More Metal Clay for Beaders*
- *Inventive Metal Clay*
- *Beautiful Wire Jewelry for Beaders*
- *Beautiful Wire Jewelry for Beaders 2*
- *Metal Clay Rings*

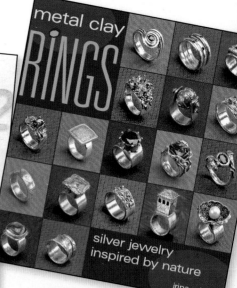